BALLET FOR BEGINNERS

FELICITY GRAY

Ballet for Beginners

by

FELICITY GRAY

WITH AN INTRODUCTION BY
CECIL McGIVERN
CONTROLLER OF TELEVISION PROGRAMMES B.B.C.
AND 106 PHOTOGRAPHS BY
GORDON ANTHONY

Also historical plates and line diagrams

PHOENIX HOUSE LIMITED
LONDON

Made 1952 in Great Britain
Printed at Plymouth by Latimer, Trend & Co Ltd
for *Phoenix House Limited*, 38 William IV Street
Charing Cross, London WC2

First published 1952
Reprinted 1952
Third impression, 1953

To my Husband
an unrepentant Balletophobe,
without whose exasperated advice I should
not have got beyond the
first paragraph

CONTENTS

LIST OF PLATES

8

LIST OF PLATES

9

DRAWINGS

INTRODUCTION

By CECIL McGIVERN
Controller of Television Programmes, B.B.C.

I AM DELIGHTED that *Ballet for Beginners* is published. It will, I am sure, further Felicity Gray's purpose, which is ballet, and mine, which is television. Ballet, particularly when it is specially arranged or specially written for television, suits the medium, and has formed part of television programmes since television began as a public service in this country in 1936. It was not popular, however, and as television began to spread across the country, reaching out from London, where ballet has long been normal theatrical entertainment, to towns and villages where ballet was seldom, if ever, seen, it began to fall lower in the programme ratings. 'Why on earth do you have so much ballet?' was a question frequently put to me, and generally in much more forcible language. That question, at a time when ballet appeared in programmes only about once a month, was a measure of ballet's unpopularity on the television screen.

However, it is television's duty to use and, if possible, to foster all forms of art and entertainment, and ballet could not be dropped from the programme schedules. The answer was obvious—to explain ballet, to show its history, its methods, its vocabulary, to demonstrate that it is not only for a minority taste, to show that everyone, with just a little effort, can appreciate its beauty and purpose. I asked Philip Bate, television producer, to start a series of programmes called *Ballet for Beginners*, and he turned at once to dancer and choreographer Felicity Gray, who had always enthusiastically preached the cause of ballet in television and who, I think, was the first choreographer to devise a ballet specially for television.

Ballet for Beginners was an immediate success. As a series of six programmes, it has been televised twice and I have no doubt that it will continue to form part of television's permanent repertoire of programmes. In the past two years, television ballet has slowly but surely climbed in popularity and it is gratifying that in 1951 two ballet programmes, *Les Sylphides* produced by Christian Simpson, and a presentation of *Les Ballets des Champs Elysées*, by Philip Bate were among the most popular programmes of the year. I am sure that an important part of the reason for this success was *Ballet for Beginners*.

Another good came out of these programmes. At first, Felicity Gray's name appeared in the credits but she herself was not seen on the screen. She wrote the scripts, rehearsed the dancers, then, during transmission, stood on the studio floor signalling to soloists, *corps de ballet*, orchestra and narrator. It was inevitable, however, that very soon she herself should become the narrator, and her charming manner and eager voice helped greatly to make the series as successful as it undoubtedly was.

I had one regret over *Ballet for Beginners*. Television programmes are ephemeral. All the thought, preparation, rehearsal, all the dancing, the costumes, the scenery—gone in less than an hour. No time for people to look and re-look, to consider, to ponder. Now this weakness has gone. Here is *Ballet for Beginners* in a more permanent form, offering time and opportunity for more leisured study. Study, however, is too hard a word. I am sure that Felicity Gray's gaiety and compelling enthusiasm have made this book as easy and delightful to read as they made *Ballet for Beginners* on the television screen attractive to watch.

AUTHOR'S NOTE

SINCE THE production of the television series Ballet for Beginners, I have received many suggestions that the material of those programmes should be put into permanent form, accessible to all 'beginners', whether dancers or audience. This book is the result. It attempts to cover a great deal of ground in a small space, so of necessity each chapter gives only the outline of the subject. Nevertheless I hope and believe that it will be a useful introduction for both students and ballet-goers.

In the descriptions of technical steps and positions I am not advocating any particular method, but describing them as they are most frequently seen on the stage. The names I have used are those employed by the Royal Academy of Dancing because they are the most widely known in this country.

I would like to thank Mr Cecil McGivern, Controller of B.B.C. Television Programmes, without whose imagination and common sense Ballet for Beginners would never have come into existence—the programme was indeed entirely his idea originally; and also Mr Philip Bate, our producer, whose knowledge of classical ballet and understanding of the special problems involved in presenting it on the television screen, were responsible for the success of the series. Others to whom I am indebted are Miss Belinda Quirey for information concerning dances at the court of Louis XIV; Mr C. W. Beaumont for his kind permission to reproduce Plates 33, 34, and 87; and last but not least, Mr Gordon Anthony for the care which he gave to the photographs.

F. G.

The dancers in the demonstration photographs are as follows:
>   Domini Callaghan and David Paltenghi: Plates 43, 46–50
>   Michel de Lutry: Plates 51–54
>   David Blair: Plate 18
>   Sonya Hana and David Blair: Plates 36–39, 41, 42, 44, 45
>   Margarita Tate: Plates 20–24, 28, 29, 63–85, 90
>   Margarita Tate and David Blair: Plate 40
>   Sonya Hana: Plates 5–8, 21–24, 29
>   Yvonne Cartier: Plates 11–14, 20, 25, 27, 28, 30
>   Marjorie Woodhams: Plates 11, 20, 26, 27
>   Hazel Wiscombe: Plates 11, 12, 25, 26

Chapter I

FEET AND LEGS

THE PRINCIPAL intention of this book is to help those who are beginning to enjoy ballet, either on the stage or on television, by explaining a little about it—just as it helps one's appreciation of a picture to know how and with what the artist painted it. It is hoped that this book will also be of help to those who contemplate taking up ballet as a career, or who are in the early stages of training.

What exactly is this ballet dancing? How does it differ from other forms of dancing? How did it all start?

Obviously, a full answer would run into many volumes. But the basic difference between classical ballet technique and all other dancing techniques is *not*, as many people think, that the dancers get on the tips of their toes (the 'points' in ballet language); it is that all steps and exercises are done 'turned out'. Turn-Out simply means one foot east, one foot west (Pl. 5). The whole leg from the hip—thigh, knee, and ankle—is turned out; whatever the step, or the position of the leg in relation to the dancer's body, it must always be 'turned out'. (Pls. 6, 7 and 8).

This position can look very odd and unnatural in the classroom. How did it come to be adopted as the basic foundation of all ballet dancing? The answer takes us back to the reign of Louis XIV of France, himself passionately fond of dancing, and a point of fashion which brought the turn-out to Court at the psychological moment.

In the early seventeenth century the cavaliers of France all wore, as the height of fashion, heavy bucket-shaped cavalry boots (Pl. 2). It was quite impossible in these boots to walk as one does to-day, brushing one leg past the other; the legs had to be swung out and round in a small arc to avoid the wide boot tops and, as the foot came to the ground, the toes quite naturally turned out. One can see something of the same style of walk to-day in fishermen who have rolled their big rubber waders down below the knee. ✓

Thus, the walk of the cavalier developed into the swagger of the Three Musketeers. Even after the fashion of these boots had passed, as fashions do, the turned-out position of the feet continued to be cultivated. You can see it in any of the paintings or prints of Court life in those days. For once the ladies followed, rather than set, the fashion; because, under the King's leadership, most of the dance steps of the day were designed to show off the men, the women had to copy the men's style, and so came to adopt the Turn-Out for themselves. In this period of history, ballroom dancing was entirely a pastime of the aristocracy and one of its most important accomplishments. A strong turn-out was the hall-mark of a good dancer and reputations were won and lost on the turn of a toe. So fashion was the first reason why the Turn-Out came to be adopted.

The second reason was efficiency. The ballroom dances of the day were based upon the Turn-Out and you couldn't perform the steps of the Minuet, the Sarabande, the Passe-pied or any other of the Court dances without employing it. The light delicate footwork in the quicker dances, the controlled balance in the slower ones, and the very subtle rhythms of them all were impossible to do unless you had gained the control which comes with a well-trained Turn-Out. It would have been like trying to ride a bicycle with no sense of balance. Because King Louis was such a keen dancer himself and gave so many entertainments, the ballroom steps became more and more complicated, and there began to grow up a definite technique. This technique was based upon the Turn-Out because it was found that such a stance gave the most control and strength, the liveliest and neatest feet, and the most upright carriage— and in the costumes of that period you had to hold yourself upright or look pretty silly.

Court etiquette was the third reason why Turn-Out came to stay. While Louis was still quite a young man, his health began to decline and his waist-line to spread; before long he was incapable of doing much dancing himself. However, he still remained an enthusiastic spectator of his own entertainments. One of the strictest rules of the Court was that no one must ever turn their back upon the King; also, we must remember that the courtiers not only danced for their own pleasure, but were the entertainers in all the spectacles designed by Louis himself (professional dancers were quite another matter and came later on). Thus, it came about, since the King was now only an onlooker, that all entertainments had to be designed to be seen from the front only, as in any theatre nowadays. Under these conditions, it was found that the Turn-Out gave the most pleasing outline to the dancers.

So there are the three main reasons for ballet's basic position—the *fashion* of bucket boots, the *efficiency* it gave to the dancing and the *etiquette* of dancing to face the King after he no longer took part himself.

Another legacy left to us by the Court of Louis XIV is the language of ballet. Since ballet originated in France, it was natural that the technical terms should be described in French, and the tradition remains to this day. This isn't just sheer historical affectation. Ballet has always been international and you will find many different nationalities represented

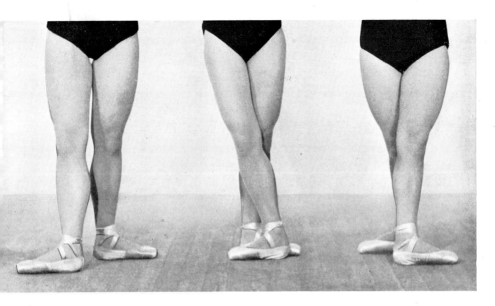

10. 4th position, *ouverte* (open); 5th, 4th *croisée* (crossed)

12. An Assemblé. Throw the leg away; jump after it; land both feet together

Both legs stretched in air

Land on one foot, close the raised leg to finish as
in A. B and C are in arabesque

14. Another kind of Sissone

Jump from both feet

13. A Sissone

Jump from 5th position

One leg bent in air, toe to knee

Land on one foot. Close raised foot straight
downwards to finish as in A

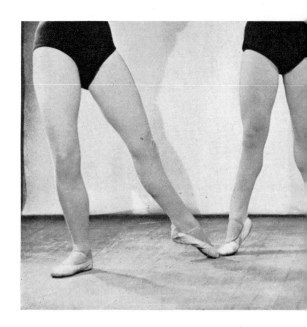

15. A Glissade. These four

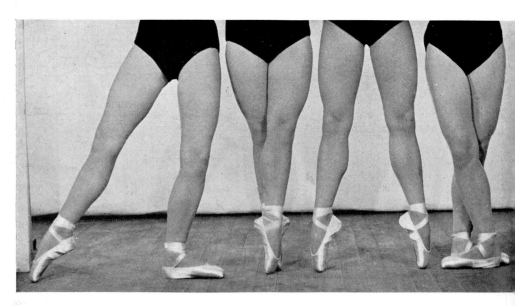

16. A Pas de Bourrée. The preparation; 5th position; 2nd position; 5th position. These four stages are clear and separate, though usually quick

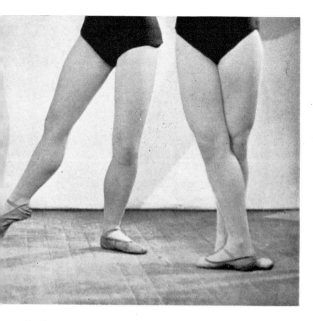

moothed into one movement

17. Another Pas de Bourrée. In the 2nd and 3rd stages the released foot is picked up to the knee

18. An example of Grande Batterie. One leg is thrown up as in A, the other joins it as in B, the dancer lands as in A

2. Left, correct; right, incorrect—shoulders have been raised with arms

3. The 'Gateway' Left, correct; right, incorrect—has slackened between the shoulder blades

24. Left, correct; right has arms too far back, which makes her chin poke forward and seat stick out

25. 1st position

THE FIVE POSITIONS
OF THE ARMS:
STRAIGHT AND WITH
EPAULEMENT

27. 3rd position

29. 5th position

in one ballet company; whatever they may wish to say to each other in private is their own affair, but it is essential to have a common language in their work, otherwise the curtain would never go up. The universal use of French to describe the steps and movements in ballet gives all dancers a sort of international language, so that they can attend classes and rehearsals in any country in the world.

It would need a long anatomical lecture to explain just why the Turn-Out gives such strength and control to a dancer's movements, but we can get a rough idea if we compare the muscles of the body with a piece of elastic. Ordinary elastic expands only in one direction, but the 'two-way stretch' kind will stretch in any direction. Ballet training develops *all* the many muscles in the human body and the effect is to give the dancer a sort of two-way stretch all over. Ordinary people do not have that sort of development, not even athletes.

It is this training, based on the Turn-Out, which enables dancers' legs to go all round their bodies without disturbing their carriage. An eminent soldier, married to a ballet dancer, once acidly remarked that a dancer was like a mule, she could kick you from all round the compass. The 'control room' lies in the hips, and if you watch a good dancer at practice you will see that, no matter where the legs go, the hips remain steady and never wiggle.

The next point to consider is the positions of the feet, of which there are five (Pls. 9 and 10).

In the 1st Position, the heels are touching, and the feet are in a straight line, pointing in opposite directions.

The 2nd Position is an open one, toes and heels still on the same base line, but the heels are separated by the length and a half of one's own foot. The weight of the body is squarely between the feet.

The 3rd Position is closed, the heel of the right foot lodged in the instep of the left, the toes pointing in opposite directions. This is possibly the most comfortable position.

The 4th Position is a cheat, because there are two kinds—the 'Open' and the 'Crossed 4th'. For the 'Open 4th' (see Pl. 10) the foot is in front of 1st Position and the heels are the same distance apart as in the 2nd. For the 'Crossed 4th' (see Pl. 10) the foot is in front of the 3rd *Position*, though still the same distance apart as in the 2nd.[1]

Lastly, the 5th Position, which is certainly the most uncomfortable.

[1] There are two opinions as to the correct placing of the feet in the Crossed 4th— 'opposite 5th' or 'opposite 3rd'. I have chosen the latter, as I consider it to be classically more correct, according to Cecchetti and Beauchamp; also, the early 5th Position was only 'heel to instep' (very like our modern 3rd Position), whereas to-day the 5th Position is 'heel to toe'. As a result, the Crossed 4th, if opposite our *modern* 5th, becomes a most difficult position to work from and is often responsible for bad placing of the hips under any but the very best teachers.

The toes are pointing in opposite directions, the right heel level with the left toe and vice versa.

These five positions remain the same, whether the legs are bent, straight, or on point (Pls. 3 and 4). There are five of them, no more and no less, because they are all that are needed to cover the circle of floor within the range of the dancer's legs; without these positions you cannot start, go through with, or finish any step in ballet. The two 'open' positions are also used when one leg is in the air; Plates 6, 7 and 8 show some of these variations.

Now we come to the steps themselves. There are innumerable recognized steps in the classics and fresh variations are being invented with every new ballet; but, very roughly, there are seven main groups.

The commonest, simplest, most fundamental of all steps is the *Jeté* (Pl. 11). It is one of the earliest of all dance steps, a spontaneous bound of joy. Children playing in the garden, jumping from one leg to the other, perform jetés. All that happens is that you throw your leg away from you, in any direction, and jump after it; or, to put it differently, you jump off one leg and land on the other. There are big (or 'grands') jetés and little jetés, like the opening phase of the Dance of the Little Swans in *Swan Lake*. Any leap, great or small, which takes off from one foot and lands on the other is a Jeté.

The *Assemblé* starts the same way. You throw your leg and jump, but you land on *both* feet (Pl. 12). The professional high-jumper performs an Assemblé, taking off from one foot and landing the other side of the bar with both feet together. Like the Jeté, the Assemblé can be done in any direction, size, or speed; but the feet always 'assemble' in the air in time to land both together in 3rd or 5th Position.

Then there is the third variety—to jump from both feet to one, bringing the other up to it (Pls. 13 a, b, c). The step ends as it begins. This is the *Sissone*, so called because it gives a scissor look to the legs while the dancer is in the air. There is the other sort of sissone, with one leg bent whilst in the air (Pls. 14 a, b, c.).

The *Temp Levé* is the common or garden hop, taking off and landing on the same foot. There is, of course, one last form of jump, to take off *and* land with both feet; but this is not worthy the distinction of a separate group, as it is not capable of as many variants as the others. The Man's Variation from the Pas-de-Trois in Act III of *Swan Lake* is a dance full of these four groups.

A dancer cannot do Jetés, Assemblés, and Sissones all the time without finishing up on the floor in a little pool of grease; some sort of linking step is needed. The most common is the *Glissade* (Pl. 15). As its name implies, it is a 'gliding' step, used mostly as a preparation for something more showy, just as one takes a run before a big jump. The Glissade joins things together, in the way that 'and', 'but', and 'or' do in speaking. It can be done in series, but is generally inserted between the bigger jumping steps.

Next comes the *Bourrée*, which is more easily recognized than described. It has two aspects—the Bourrée, a fast travelling run on point (or half-point) with tiny steps; and the Pas de Bourrée, which is three small steps in any direction, usually fast, always neat, done either with straight knees, or picking the feet well up (Pls. 16 and 17). The Bourrée is nearly always given to girls, because it looks so much better on point; for reasons which we will discuss in another chapter the male dancer almost never goes on full point, that is right on the tips of his toes. A typical variation of these basic steps is the Pas de Bourrée Renversée, in which the leg goes round the body from front to back, the body bends away from it, and untwists with a little turning Pas de Bourrée.

Lastly, there is the *Pirouette*, which is quite unmistakable. Any series of turns or spins is in fact a sort of pirouette, and one may travel as one turns, just as a top travels as it spins. Pirouettes may be done fast or slow; in any position; on full point by girls, on half-point by men; with the leg straight or the knee bent. A curious fact about pirouettes is that they are nearly always performed to the right; it is very rare to find a dancer who spins equally well to right or left. It's like the old argument about the way the water goes down the goggle; everybody knows it is so, but nobody can explain just why without a lengthy discussion. If you watch a dancer closely during a series of pirouettes, you will notice a quick flick of the head at the end of each turn; this not only helps the turn, but also prevents the dancer getting dizzy by fixing the eyes on one spot. To get the idea, stand in front of a mirror and turn round on your toes, keeping the eyes fixed on your reflection for as long as possible; then turn your head quickly over the other shoulder and watch yourself complete the circle. But don't try it too fast to begin with!

So much for our seven, very arbitrary, groups of steps. One cannot leave them, however, without mentioning *Batterie*. Batterie is a general term, used to describe the embroidery of a jumping step. When both feet are off the ground, the legs are beaten together in mid-air, giving a sort of quivering or fluttering effect. One can 'beat' any number of times, depending on the strength of the dancer. The male dancer uses a lot of Batterie in his big jumps and this is known as 'grande batterie' (Pls. 18a and b show a cabriole); the small, twinkling, stage-skimming batterie used mostly by girls is called 'petite batterie'.

The famous *Entrechat* comes under the heading of Batterie. Here the legs are crossed as many times as the dancer can manage in the height of his or her jump. Entrechats are qualified as 'quatre', 'six', 'huit', etc.,

19

according to the number of times the legs are crossed in mid-air. The record is so far held by the almost legendary Nijinsky with an 'entre-chat dix'.

One can't do better than to wind up this chapter on Feet and Legs by dealing with the question of dancing 'sur les pointes', on the tips of toes. Dancing on points was created solely to give the effect of lightness, and is used almost exclusively by girls; as I have already explained, only on very rare occasions has a man ever gone 'on point' on the stage.

Point work is not such an unnatural thing as some believe. Ballet training makes for very strong feet, and all pointwork really means is that the dancer's feet are strong enough to support her body on the tips of her toes. Nowadays, the special blocked and stiffened ballet shoe assists the dancer to stay on tiptoe, but the first pointwork was done in shoes with no stiffening at all.

We will deal with the construction of the ballet shoe in the last chapter; all that need be said here is that, for pointwork, the most important part of the modern shoe is the special stiffening along the sole and instep, rather than the papier maché blocking on the toe (Pl. 89). All ballet shoes are hand made and they vary considerably in quality and fitting. Often one performance of a strenuous classical role, such as Odette in *Swan Lake*, is as much as one pair of shoes can stand; although, like human beings, some wear better than others. However great a ballerina may be, she will always attend to her shoes herself. No one else can be trusted even to sew on the ribbons; they must be in exactly the right place to hold the shoe firmly without pulling over the instep.

A student has nine months to a year of hard daily training in un-blocked shoes before she is allowed her first pair of 'points'; and even then these are only used for a few minutes a day in simple exercises. Many a young dancer's feet have been ruined by going on point before the muscles were strong enough to support the weight of her body. Finally, all new ballet shoes have to be 'broken in' before they are used in performance, for a period varying between one morning and two days.

This chapter deals, very broadly, with the work of the feet and legs, but feet and legs are only one half of the story. A dancer's instrument is the whole body and the upper half is just as important as the lower. Brilliant footwork may dazzle you, but bad arms will take away all the grace and magic; equally, the most beautiful arms cannot hide unsteady balance or clumsy feet. In the next chapter it will be seen how much the arms, shoulders, and head contribute to the total effect.

Chapter II

ARMS AND HEAD

MANY PEOPLE think that ballet dancing is 'all legs' and that the upper half of the body has little to do with the finished result. This couldn't be more untrue. The technique of feet and legs is the scaffolding, as it were, upon which the dancer builds, and it is the upper half of the body which is the interpretative, expressive part. One of the earliest ballet masters said that 'the Arms should be to the Body what the frame is to the picture'.

Just as the Turn-Out is peculiar to ballet, so there is a special way of holding the arms which does not apply to any other form of dancing. Plate 19 is the lithograph of the famous Pas de Quatre of 1845, when the four most famous ballerinas of the day—Taglioni, Grisi, Cerrito, and Lucille Grahn—danced before Queen Victoria. You will notice how softly the arms are curved, with no signs of strain anywhere.

First, then, let us deal with the way the arms are *held* in classical ballet. When the arm is down, the elbow is held away from the body and it stays in that curve, wherever the arm may be moved: the wrist and elbow follow the same curve. Above all, there must be no angles anywhere (Pls. 20–29). Elbows must never intrude on the line by dropping in to the waist or by stiffening; nor must a dancer ever remind one of a prize-fighter, with hunched shoulders. Plates 21–24 show some of the horrible results of holding the arms the wrong way. When the arms rise, the elbows keep the same position. They should feel supported underneath and must not drop into an angle or stiffen. The same thing applies when the arms are above the head—no corners, no stiffening, no dragging forward. In all these positions, there is one gentle line through the back of the hand, the wrist, the point of the elbow to the shoulder; this curve must always look just right and be adjusted to the individual proportions of each dancer.

As for the hand itself, it must provide a decorative finish to the line of the arm without calling undue attention to itself. 'Overconscious' or 'unconscious' hands are equally bad—they resemble either a cactus or a bunch of bananas.

The *movement* of the arms in ballet is called *Port-de-bras* (carriage of the arms), and in a dancer's training there are five rules for its use.

First, the arm must move freely from the shoulder, without disturbing it, just as the legs move without disturbing the body; a dancer's neckline must never be spoilt by the shoulder rising with the arm (Pl. 22) or by letting go between the shoulder blades when the arms are in front (Pl. 23).

Second, the arms must never go behind the neck and shoulders; when the dancer looks straight ahead with the arms raised, both arms should be visible out of the corner of the eye. If they get behind the head, the effect is to poke the neck forward like an inquisitive hen's (Pl. 24).

Third, the arms move *up* in front of the body and *down* at the sides.

Fourth, they never cross an imaginary line down the centre of the body.

Fifth, they must always pass through the 'Gateway' (Pl. 23a), on their way to any other position. The Gateway is exactly the same as the 5th Position of the arms, except that it is opposite the diaphragm. This is a most important aspect of a dancer's training, and its function as a sort of clearing house for all the arm movements gives a grace and coherence to everything the dancer does with his or her arms.

Just like the Turn-Out, this distinctive carriage and movement of the arms had its origin and grew up in the court of Louis XIV (Pl. 31). The tight, boned bodices of the women and the equally tight doublets of the men compelled them to hold themselves very upright. The heavy sleeves kept the elbows away from the waist, both for convenience and because they were seen to better advantage that way. The complicated coiffures and wigs made them turn their heads slowly and graciously, with no tossing or bending (if you read an historical novel of that period in which the heroine 'tosses her pretty head', don't you believe it!). The swinging cloaks of the men gave them a natural swagger, with shoulders back and chests puffed out. In those clothes it was quite impossible to stand in the relaxed manner that we do to-day.

From the time of Louis XIV until late into the eighteenth century, the function of the arms in dancing was simply to balance the body; the natural opposition of right-foot left-hand, such as we use in walking, was as strictly enforced as is the rule of contrary body movement in modern ballroom dancing. The arm movements were purely utilitarian and the upper arm was never raised above shoulder level, largely because the dressmaking of that time would not permit it. It was not until after the French Revolution that the arms began to be used as a decoration, to enhance the beauty of the dance, and to make lines and pictures of their own.

Owing to this 'austerity' in the use of the arms, there were only three recognized movements in King Louis's day. The first was a simple change of opposition to balance the body; a comparison between the arms positions in Pl. 33 and Pl. 39 will show how this was adopted into classical ballet and became 2nd Position of the arms. The second movement was a 'circling' of the forearm; the circle was always described inwards, upwards, and outwards and to this gesture we owe the rule 'Up in front, down at the sides'. The third movement, a quick flick of the wrist to mark a jump and to show off one's lace ruffles, has left no mark on ballet. However, the gesture of self-presentation to the King is practically the same in ballet to-day and is known as 'demi-bras' (Pl. 20b).

So fashion, efficiency, and etiquette played their part in the development of the port-de-bras in classical ballet, just as they did with the feet and legs. When the earliest ballet masters came to work out the technique of this new, young art, they naturally made use of the dance movements of their day and elaborated them, so producing a formula which governs all ballet to-day. Ballet is a very young branch of the arts, only three hundred years old. But it's a thoroughly healthy child, even if sometimes alarmingly precocious; and while its traditions live it will always be able to look after itself.

As with the feet, so there are Five Arm Positions in ballet, which might be described as the starting and stopping places of all arm movements. Unlike the feet, the arm positions have several variations; but the five shown in Pls. 26–30 are derived from the French.[1] Arm positions are completely independent of feet positions and any arm position can be used in conjunction with any position of the feet, body, or head.

In addition to the five arm positions, there are three more which are known by names and no numbers. These are *Bras bas, Demi-bras* and *Bras croisé*.

BRAS BAS, 'arms down' (Pl. 20a) is the position from which many arm movements start; the palms are facing each other and the hands slightly curved—it's really the 5th Position of the Arms upside down.

DEMI-BRAS, 'half arms' (Pl. 20b) lineal descendant from the court of King Louis, is very useful because of its feeling of appeal to the audience.

BRAS CROISÉ, 'crossed arm' (Pl. 20c), is used as a preparation for pirouettes; it is the strong, swift opening of the crossed arm, together with the inward and downward motion of the extended arm, which gives impetus to the turn.

The use of the arms can be given infinite variation and expression with the aid of the body and shoulders. It is *Epaulement*, the use of the head, body, and shoulders, which gives flavour and character to what are in all eight very simple arm positions. Plates 26–30 also show how the arm positions can be enhanced by Epaulement; a little change in the angle and carriage of the shoulders, a slight bend in the body, and the whole atmosphere of a position is altered.

[1] These are the positions used by the Royal Academy of Dancing.

There is one very familiar sight in ballet which is neither a position nor a step, but which cannot be ignored. It is in fact a line, and is in a class of its own. This is the *Arabesque*. To put it baldly, when the dancer's leg is stretched straight behind the body, that is an Arabesque; it is a line which reaches from the extended foot, through the arched back, to the shoulder. The arms can be in any position and it is still called an Arabesque, although the pure classical Arabesque continues the line to the ends of the fingers as in Pl. 30; there are many more varieties of Arabesques shown in the accompanying photographs.

Upon all these strictly defined positions and movements, the dancer imposes his or her own personality and that of the character portrayed in the ballet. Within the strict style of classical ballet, the suggestion of character depends very largely on the dancer's powers of interpretation. An Arabesque, for instance, can be just a very beautiful line, or it can convey a world of pity and sorrow, or yet again be the most joyous thing on earth, all according to the character of a role and the artistry of a dancer. An Arabesque, a Position, a Step remain in principle the same in any ballet; it is by detail that the feeling of character is conveyed, detail in the way in which the hands are used, details in the phrasing of an arm movement. It is such attention to detail that differentiates between, say, the Swan Queen in *Swan Lake* and the Blue Bird in *Sleeping Princess*. The actual range of steps and movements in the old classics is surprisingly small.

It is very hard to be definite when writing of the arms, because the phrase 'rules are made to be broken' is appallingly true of the art of ballet from the waist upward. The truth is that there is only one rule that must *not* be broken and that is that the arms must never show strain, not even in the little finger.

There is one aspect which ballet has in common with sport. The principle of 'follow through' is every bit as important as it is in tennis or golf or boxing. Every movement must be fully rounded and finished, it must follow through; if it's cut short, or if the arm is forgotten halfway through, the whole dance becomes as untidy and unsatisfying as the sight of a batsman who pokes instead of drives. In dancing, even the eyes must follow through. A wrong glance can take all the feeling out of a movement, and the most gracious gesture in the world will seem boorish if the dancer is looking away, or taking a quick peek to see where she has to go next.

Timing is equally important, just as in sport. When you take off for a leap, the arms help to swing you up: when you come down, the arms descend a fraction slower to cover any possible jar. The arms assist the dancer to turn, to balance, to jump; the wrong use of them results in staggering pirouettes, wobbly arabesques, and jumps which seem (and are) full of effort. Everything works together in ballet—arms, legs, feet, hands, body, heart, and brain. That sounds a tall order and some readers may dispute 'brain', but if they reach the end of this book I hope they will admit that brains also are necessary.

To sum up, it is the feet, legs, and back which provide the strength in ballet dancing, and it is through the arms, body, and head that dancers prove their artistry and ability. Anybody with a reasonable shape, possessed of sufficient energy and ambition, can attain a very good technique; but it is the upper half of the body which shows the dancer up as someone who can merely perform certain technicalities very well, or which proves him or her to be someone who can express feeling, emotion, and character through dancing.

Chapter III

THE MALE DANCER

It is a popular misconception that the Male Dancer in classical ballet is just an elegant weight-lifter or an animated piece of scenery. Some people even ask whether male dancers, like wartime train journeys, are 'really necessary'; they regard it as a namby-pamby job for a man.

There is nothing namby-pamby about the profession of dancer, male or female. During the war, a celebrated dancer found himself the butt of a very tough P.T. sergeant in the R.A.F., who thought that all male dancers must be sissy; the sergeant was considerably shaken when, on the command 'Hands on hips, small jumps, commence', the despised recruit leapt higher, swifter, and longer than anybody else and, long after the rest of the squad was completely exhausted, he was still happily soaring up and down, throwing in an *entrechat* or two for good measure.

In the ballet, as with Adam and Eve, the Man came first. Louis XIV of France was the first person to organize ballet, when he founded the Royal Academy of Dance in 1661. In all subsequent ballets at the Paris Opéra, the women's parts were taken by men, as in our own Shakespearian theatre, and it was not until about twenty years later that professional women dancers appeared in ballet for the first time. Even fifty-two years after the foundation of the Royal Academy, that is, in 1713, the Opéra Company contained twelve male dancers, but only ten women; the ladies' combined salaries came to rather less than two-thirds of the budget for the men. In other words, the men were the stars.

One reason for this unchallenged male supremacy is to be found in the stage costume of the time. Plates 33 and 34 show M. Ballon and Mlle Subligny, a male star and ballerina of about 1703. The lady may look delightful, but her costume gives her very little chance to do anything spectacular. The men, being free from the heavy period skirts, had a far greater variety of steps at their disposal, so they did all the hard dancing and the ladies provided the charm.

The reign of the male dancer lasted about 160 years. It was Marie Taglioni who finally shattered his supremacy in 1832. The lithograph (Pl. 35) is symbolic of the change which came over the status of the male dancer; Taglioni's partner looks as if he knew what was coming to him. Taglioni herself is wearing a costume on the lines of the long, misty ballet frock which we know to-day; there is nothing about that frock to prevent dancing, and dance Taglioni certainly did.

From then onwards it was the ballerinas who claimed the lion's share of glamour and publicity. The male dancers gradually became mere supporters, nothing but weight-lifters for the ballerinas and concessions to the plot of a ballet. The lowest ebb of their career was reached at the turn of the century in Paris, and in the Alhambra and Empire Theatres in London, when the parts of the young heroes and Princes were played by girls, just as in any pantomime. The men were allowed to take only character parts or aged fathers and villains.

But the story was brought full circle when the Russian Ballet of Diaghileff burst upon Paris in 1909. Before Diaghileff, Europe had forgotten that ballets could be truly virile and that male dancers could be great and exciting artists. In the Ballets Russes, male dancers were starred equally with ballerinas. Nijinsky was the foremost and most famous, and he and his companions reinstated the male dancer with a bang. Since then, equal partnership of ballerina and male dancer has been kept.

In the early stages, ballet training is much the same for both men and girls. They are taught the turn-out, and they all do the same exercises to develop it. Both sexes need strong straight backs, strong feet and legs, suppleness, and control. But anatomically, both in bone and muscle, a man is made differently from a girl and, because of this difference in physique, he has different qualities and limitations.

For instance, his insteps are seldom as high or as supple as a girl's and he is not expected to go on points. Pl. 36 shows the normal difference in insteps. The strength in his feet is used for bigger jumps, not pointwork. This means that he can use more pirouettes and a greater variety of them. Since he is 'excused' pointwork, he has almost half his foot to turn on: the girl's balancing surface in a pirouette is no more than the blocked point of her ballet shoe, whereas the man has the whole ball of his foot (Pl. 36). Consequently, the man can 'play' with his balance by flexing the knee and ankle; but the girl, because she must have a rigid leg for a pirouette on full point, cannot so adjust her balance, and if she is unsteady there is not much she can do about it. Another difference is that a man does not bend so far back or so far forward as a girl (Pls. 37 and 38). Nor do his legs go so high (Pl. 39). Generally speaking, too, a man moves more slowly but jumps much higher, jumping more softly and with more stamina than a girl. He travels about the stage more, covering the ground with fewer steps. He bends his body about less, but spends more time in the air, using a lot of *Batterie* (Pl. 18 and 32).

As for *Port-de-Bras*, the carriage of his arms must be graceful, with a firm, flowing movement, but not for an instant must he sacrifice his masculine quality. A man who uses his arms 'daintily' is unworthy of the name of male dancer.

The contributions of the male dancer and ballerina to a ballet may be compared with those of the hands of a pianist. The training, with its scales and exercises, is much the same for both hands; but when it comes to playing a piece of music, one hand plays bass and the other treble and each is complementary to the other. So it is with dancers.

Early in his career, the male dancer discovers to which branch of his art he is best suited. There are three avenues open to him in classical ballet—Danseur Noble, Cavalier, and Danseur de Caractère.

The *Danseur Noble* takes the romantic parts, the Princes (frequently disguised), the Siegfrieds and Albrechts and noble young heroes. These roles contain some of the most brilliant solo work to be seen in classical ballet.

Besides showing off on his own, he must of course partner the ballerina, and this forms the second branch of a male dancer's work, the *Cavalier*. A Cavalier must never obtrude his own personality on that of the ballerina. When he supports her in balances, pirouettes, or lifts, he must do so unobtrusively and with great courtesy, effacing himself entirely so that she may shine. The role of Cavalier is very definitely an art on its own, as any ballerina will tell you. Skilful Cavaliers are very much in demand. But whereas a Danseur Noble must also be a Cavalier, a Cavalier does not necessarily have to be a highly accomplished Danseur Noble.

The Cavalier's is a difficult and, at times, dangerous occupation, calling not only for strength and skill but also for a certain amount of psychology. A ballerina may be difficult or easy to partner, anxious or trusting, but it is always the man's fault if the pas-de-deux is a mess! This may sound hard, but the male dancer who remembers it has the makings of a first-class Cavalier.

Take an ordinary Straight Lift, to start with. Anybody who tries to lift his wife or girl friend high in the air, and at the same time elegantly, will realize just how difficult it is. It's not only strength that counts, it's timing. The man must time his lift so as to catch the girl just at the top of her jump, in that split second before she comes down again, thus making his upward movement a continuation of her jump. If he lifts too soon, he creates an impression of effort; if he leaves it too late, she looks like a sack of coals; but if he times it just right she soars upward like a piece of thistledown on the wind (Pl. 40). Of course, the girl must jump straight. If she jumps backwards, she stands a fair chance of knocking her partner flat: if she takes off too far forward, she drops out of his hands like an escaping fish. One last point—if you watch a straight lift closely, you will see how the man gets *under* his partner's weight and pushes up a little from the thighs, thus using all his body and not just the arms alone.

Then there is the Travelling Lift. Here, the ballerina starts with a jeté;

her partner lifts her and carries her, setting her down several feet away from where she took off (Pl. 41). In addition to the problems of the Straight Lift troubles, the Cavalier now has that of setting her down at such an angle that she can balance and start the next step easily. He does this by tilting her from the waist so that she can get her foot on the ground gracefully. Here again, nice judgment is required—tilt her too far forward and she can't reach the ground (Pl. 42); too far backward and both her feet touch down simultaneously, making her look like a pair of dividers. And of course, all this must be done at exactly the right moment in the music. Putting down is as important as lifting up; a little carelessness in setting a ballerina straight on to her points can wreck her feet for the rest of the performance, besides leading to a lot of unpleasantness in the dressing-room afterwards.

Another headache for the Cavalier is the Supported Balance on Point, which forms such a large part of any classical pas-de-deux (Pl. 43). It looks simple enough to the audience; all the work seems to be done by the ballerina, poised as she is on one leg on point, turning gracefully, and finally left to balance for a moment on her own. Certainly, it is a showpiece for the ballerina and is often employed at the loudest parts of the music, in order to indicate just what a feat it is. But the Cavalier holds her success in his hands. Whether he is supporting her by her hand, her elbow, or the waist, whether she is turning under his arm or he is turning her by walking round her, he must keep his eyes fixed on his ballerina, watching for the slightest sign of insecurity, ready to adjust her balance. When walking round her, a clumsy step or a loose wrist will make her fall off point at once; he must never fidget with his feet and he must keep his eyes fixed on one spot—the ballerina. No man can make a dancer steady if she is off balance, but a poor partner can prevent the most rocklike ballerina from looking secure.[1]

Next there is the question of pirouettes. Catching pirouettes well is the very devil. The girl turns inside her partner's hands and his right hand controls her speed, either acting as a brake or helping her round. If she inclines a little to either side, or too far back, or too far forward, he corrects her with a gentle push—not so easy as it sounds when she is turning fast (Pl. 44). He stops her after a set number of turns or, by prior agreement, after 'as many turns as we can do' (note the significant 'we'). Woe betide the Cavalier who stops his ballerina after three turns when she could have done four! Moreover, it is quite amazingly easy to stop

---

[1] The most difficult and famous example of this work is in the 'Rose Adagio' from the Act I of the *Sleeping Princess*. It starts in the position held by Domini Callaghan and David Paltenghi in Plate 43. Four Princes in turn walk the Ballerina round once each. She never comes off point, and as each Prince leaves, she takes her hand up to 5th and down again on to the hand of the next Prince. If the ballerina is unsteady it is more than likely to be the fault of one or more of the four Cavaliers.

your partner facing in the wrong direction; this not only looks odd but leads to considerable trouble with the ballerina. All this time the Cavalier must remain unostentatiously good to look at; the hunched shoulders, anxious face, ready hands, and straddled stance of a rugger forward waiting to tackle will not go down at all well with the balleto- manes (Pl. 45). Nor must the audience ever see more than is necessary of the Cavalier's hands on the ballerina's waist as he controls her pir- ouettes; the forearm must never appear, if it does the immediate effect is that of an indelicate hug.

A pirouette which comes at the end of the Grand Pas-de-Deux in Act II of *Swan Lake* is the Finger Fouetté. Here the ballerina takes hold of her partner's forefinger, and he keeps her turning on point by a gentle stirring motion of the arm. He must stir on a strictly vertical pivot, or he will stir her right off balance; likewise she must not hold on to his finger too hard (as a nervous dancer is liable to do), because she will then hurt him considerably. The 'preparation' for this movement must be smooth and unnoticeable. What must never be seen is the man carefully presenting his finger to the girl and the girl taking a quick look to see that it is there (Pls. 46 and 47).

The most spectacular and most difficult of all the classical double- work pirouettes is the one known as 'The Fish', which comes in the pas-de-deux between Aurora and her Prince in the last Act of *Sleeping Princess*. It is difficult to describe, horribly difficult to do, but very lovely to see when done well. The girl takes a preparation on her partner's arm (Pl. 48); she does her pirouette unsupported and finishes in Arab- esque. Her partner immediately takes her round the waist and pulls her forward; simultaneously she lifts the leg she is standing on up to the other one. He tilts her sharply downward till her head is well below her heels, wedges her between knee and arm (apparently not supporting her at all), while she arches her back and looks as though she liked it (Pl. 49). Then he swings her up again into a straight lift but without touching the floor (Pl. 50) and sets her down ready to repeat it. The whole thing takes a quarter of the time it does to tell and, when learning it, it is convenient to forget that the floor is hard.

The secret of the good Cavalier is that he is hardly noticed. His job should appear so easy that it is taken for granted. His title is a literal translation of his behaviour towards his ballerina; he treats her with deference, courtesy, and admiration, always putting her before himself. In the big classical roles, this is not made any easier by the fact that he has to change at a moment's notice from the self-effacing Cavalier into the brilliant, spectacular Danseur Noble for his own solo and, immediately the ballerina needs his support, back to the Cavalier again.

Now we come to the third part of a male dancer's job, *Danseur de*

Caractère. Character dancing in classical ballet covers a wide range of Old Men, Funny Men, and Bad Men (including thwarted lovers and magicians) and an important section can be grouped under the heading of 'national', those very energetic dances based on the folk-dancing of various lands and adapted for the stage. The latter can be performed by both men and girls but all the most exciting, showy steps go to the men; they provide the fireworks on such occasions, while the girls provide the decoration. Many of the steps, such as jumping over your own leg, touching your toes, or clicking your heels in the air, or the Cobbler (sitting on your heels and shooting out each leg in turn) (Pls. 51, 52, 53, 54) are practised separately as part of a male dancer's training, just as pointwork is part of a girl's training. These distinctive male steps, many of them based on Russian folk-dancing, are quite outside the range of a girl's capabilities; it's not that she couldn't do them if she tried but that, in doing them, she would develop a fine crop of bulging muscles, because she is not built to take that kind of strain. The Dance of the Three Ivans from *Sleeping Princess*, the Polovtsian Men's Dance in *Prince Igor*, the Buffon from *Casse-Noisette*, and the Miller's Dance in *Three-Cornered Hat* are typical examples of this 'national' style of character dancing, although the last of them is not officially a classic yet since its choreographer, Léonide Massine, is still very much alive.

In passing, it is worth mentioning that there is one famous Character Dance which is a girl's role—the Dance of the Polovtsian Girl in *Prince Igor*. This dance calls for a compact speed and agility outside the range of a man. It is a most startling and invigorating solo when danced well (Pl. 55).

It is important to remember that a male dancer is never expected to excel in all three categories at once, although of course the Danseur Noble and the Cavalier are allied.

There is a fourth category which developed after the era of classical ballet and which is now universally recognized. This is *Demi-Caractère* or 'half-character'. Examples are to be found amongst the girl's roles in the classical ballets, particularly Swanhilda's solo in Act II of *Coppélia*, but it was the great choreographer Fokine who gave it the status it enjoys to-day. Demi-Caractère work is a link between Danseur Noble and Danseur de Caractère and is based upon classical technique; but the whole style is devised to fit the character portrayed in the ballet rather than to be a display of pure technical accomplishment. The dances of Harlequin in Fokine's *Carnaval* (Pls. 56, 57 and 58) for instance, are all composed of jetés, assemblés, pirouettes, and other classical steps but they are intended to be danced as Fokine imagined that Harlequin himself would have danced them; the whole ballet is perfect demi-caractère. As far as the actual steps go, Demi-Caractère dances *could* be danced in

31

the straight classical style; but if they were, they would lose all their point—they would, in fact, lose their character.

Few people realize that the life of a male dancer is very hard and sometimes perilous. Many a Cavalier's black eye or lost tooth is the fault of a ballerina with windmills instead of arms. There is a mental as well as a physical strain, for apart from the anxiety of his own performance the main responsibility for the ballerina's performance rests with her partner. Above all, whatever he does, however hard or energetic his dances, he must soar through the evening, disguising all sense of strain. That is what separates dancers from athletes. Compare Plate 59 with Plate 60; the athlete may be breaking records, but he doesn't have to pretend that it's as easy as kiss-your-hand. Both men put all their strength into their respective performances, but a dancer's strength must be distributed through his whole body, even to the face and finger-tips, because no part of him must give away the effort.

Which gives you the most pleasure to look at?

38. A man is not expected to bend as far as a girl

39. A man's legs do not go as high as a girl's

42. The cavalier has tilted his partner at the wrong angle in this travelled lift

41. A travelled lift

40. A straight lift

48. Preparation for the 'fish' pirouette. An arabesque on the cavalier's arm, preparatory to the pirouette

49. The pirouette has been done, and finishes like this

er up in a straight lift, and
peat the pirouette

52. Touching toes in the air

51. Jumping over your own leg

56, 57, 58. Michel de Lutry in the demi-caractère
part of Harlequin in *Carnaval*

59. Harold Turner in *The Blue Bird*

Sport and General Photograph

60. A. S. Paterson, athlete, performing a high jump

62. Domini Callaghan and David Paltenghi in *Giselle*

61. Domini Callaghan and David Paltenghi in Act II, *Swan Lake*. The Prince's position means 'protect', Odette's 'thank you'

Chapter IV

MIME

MIME IS THE oldest form of expression in the world; its origins go back beyond coherent speech. Even to-day, we make use of mime, when we meet a foreigner who doesn't understand English, when we play Dumb Crambo, or that exciting American import known as 'the Game'.

Mime is simply a sign language, and classical ballet uses it to tell its very complicated stories. No language is much use if only the person speaking it can understand it; though one may pick up a word here and there which sounds the same in English, the general sense is entirely lost. It is the same with mime. We all know how infuriated we get in party games when our friends fail to understand our desperate gesticulations and grimaces.

Similarly, the passages of mime in classical ballet tend to become boring and very irritating. We can gather roughly what is going on, but it all seems much too long and much too static. In the opening of Act II of *Swan Lake*, for example, there is an exchange of mime between the Swan Queen and the Prince, in which it is easy enough to gather that she is entreating him not to shoot and he is promising he won't; but, as you will see from the full conversation given on page 38, there's a lot more to it than that. If we could only understand the whole conversation, it would at least save us from crouching between the seats trying to read the programme notes by the light of a match.

First, let's consider how mime and ballet came to join forces at all.

The history of mime is an enormously complicated subject. For once, Louis XIV had little to do with it, for mime was established as a major theatrical art in Roman times. In the sixteenth and seventeenth centuries, it was flourishing in many countries, and no doubt each country had its own home-grown vocabulary of signs. In England, the mime spectacles to be seen at Drury Lane under Mr Weaver were probably far ahead of anything the Continent had to offer at that time; but unfortunately there is little evidence to show that they affected the ballet that was growing up in Paris in any way, and that is what concerns us.

The 'sponsor' of mime in ballet was the Italian tradition of the Commedia dell'Arte. This untranslatable phrase describes a lusty and popular kind of show which emerged from Italy in the fifteenth century, a sort of mediaeval ancestor to the music hall. Unlike the select and highbrow shows enjoyed by the Princes and dukes in their own private theatres, it was entirely a people's entertainment, and was originally performed in the market places and public squares.

Comedy, farce, slapstick, clowning, pure improvisation, or 'gagging' were all part of the Commedia dell'Arte, and mime, song, and dance were all used. Because it relied so much on mime and clowning and tumbling, it developed an international appeal, and companies of strolling players spread from Italy all through Europe. In foreign countries the Italian players relied more and more on mime to get their stories, jokes, and sentiments across to the audience. Finally, we find a Commedia dell'Arte company occupying a theatre in Paris just at the time that ballet was developing at the Court.

The Commedia dell'Arte has influenced every branch of art, literature and the theatre. For example, think how many of its characters are still with us to-day—Harlequin, in his uniform of diamond checks which were originally the patches in his shabby costume; Columbine; Pierrot; Mr. Punch of *Punch and Judy*; even the costumes and make-up of many of our clowns.

For quite a long time after Louis XIV had founded his Royal Academy of Dancing, ballet remained aloof in its aristocratic circles, and continued to explain its plots with songs, introduced between the dances. Then, in 1708, the Duchesse du Maine gave an entertainment in her château which was the presentation of a tragic play acted solely in mime.

It was performed by two of the principal dancers from the Paris Opéra and caused a sensation. Mime was suddenly recognized by the ballet world, and gradually began to supplant songs for the telling of the plot. By the nineteenth century, ballet consisted of both dancing and mime. The ballet audiences were still composed mainly of the aristocracy, who were themselves amateur dancers of considerable skill, and who now learned mime at the same time as their dancing; so the audiences understood the language of mime when it was used on the stage.

During the twentieth century, the public for ballet has grown wider and wider. It no longer consists solely of connoisseurs. Consequently, the mime scenes are nowadays often cut or slurred over, in the hope that the audience has already read the story in the programme. But if one knows what the dancers' gestures mean, then the mime scenes become as fascinating as the dances, and the plot becomes clearer than any programme note can make it.

Mime gestures can be divided into two categories—practical, that is any gesture easily recognizable because it is common sense, gestures that anybody might make to a companion on the other side of the street or when speaking through a window; and formal, those gestures which are traditional signs and just have to be learnt.

Formal gestures are rather like the road signs in the Highway Code.

Who knows what a triangle or a torch stuck up on a pole by the side of the road indicates until the meaning is explained to them? Yet there is logic behind the road signs; the torch of learning is a reasonable enough sign for a school, once you know about torches of learning. Similarly, there is usually the same sort of logic behind the formal mime gestures. For instance, royalty is denoted by what at first seems to be a general flapping of the hands round the head; but these movements are, in fact, outlining a crown and, after a bit, one realizes that 'king' and 'queen' are indicated with two hands, while 'prince' or 'princess' employ only one. It is all quite logical once you *know*! Not so long ago my husband caused a shocked stir in Convent Garden, during a mime scene in *Sleeping Princess*, by asking in a loud voice whether the Queen was asking her son if he had washed behind the ears; he now knows enough to understand that she was telling him that he must give up his wild ways and choose a bride at the ball that evening.

It is these *formal* mime gestures which have come down to us from the Commedia dell'Arte. There are slight complications, due to the fact that some gestures have several meanings and one has to guess which meaning is intended from the context and the manner or expression with which it is performed. For instance, Plates 85 a, b, c, and d illustrate 'who?', 'how?', 'what?', 'where?' and 'why'?; exactly the same gesture is used for them all, but it is surprisingly easy to interpret it correctly in a mime scene that is well played. In the same way, shaking the clenched fists above the head means either a 'wizard', a 'bad, or wicked person' or 'anger'.

Then there are the words which can be done in two ways. For instance, 'dance', as a gentle, romantic character would act it, is a gentle movement through 5th Position. But a peasant character would do a 'step hop' twice instead of the graceful port-de-bras. This is quite in order—after all, one doesn't expect a farm labourer to talk with a public school accent!

Last among the formal mime snags there are those gestures which are nearly alike and yet mean totally different things. Plate 80a shows 'but' (or 'if'), 80b 'perhaps', 80c is 'one' (numeral). Plate 71 shows 'here' (or 'come here') as an order, and also the order 'obey'. In every case a slight turn of the wrist alters the meaning completely. Done carelessly or watched carelessly, these can be very confusing.

All mime gestures must be unhurried and done with conviction. They must be very exact and as simple as possible. This is by no means as easy as it sounds when one has to keep in time to the music and in character with one's role.

There is only one golden rule about mime—anything is permissible so long as it is clear to the audience, including those furthest away. But the audience must play its part and learn the traditional *formal* gestures. Remember that, when these classical ballets were first presented eighty to a hundred years ago, most of the audience 'learnt the language' as a matter of course. To-day formal mime is used less and less to tell the story and it is only in the classical ballets that one finds passages of conversation in the old-style mime, quite separate from the dancing.

The grammar of mime may seem odd when literally translated: 'You me paid not why?' 'You me shoot not please' and so on. This is due partly to the fact that sentences are still put together according to French grammar (as they were when first used in ballet), and also because the gestures must be arranged to the music and, like the dance steps, must fit the musical phrase as well as following each other smoothly and beautifully. Syntax comes a very poor second to all these priorities! Understanding mime sentences is rather like reading back someone else's shorthand.

Just as there is character dancing, so there is character mime. In the same way that an actor may speak the same lines in different dialects, so the dancer will make mime gestures in the manner in which the character he is portraying would make them. For this reason character mime may be harder to understand than straight mime, but a dancer must be careful not to overdo the character and so make the mime unintelligible, just as an actor must not be carried away by a Scots or Yorkshire part until a London audience doesn't know what he's talking about. An over-enthusiastic character dancer in a mime sequence can become incomprehensible, not only to the audience, but even to the other dancers on the stage.

In the television programmes which were the origin of this book, Tom McCall set to music a variation of the old nursery rhyme and we called it 'The House That Man Built', using as many mime gestures as possible, both formal and practical. Here is the final verse:

> I KNOW the WIZARD, who then went MAD
> To SEE the QUEEN GIVE ALL she had
> To her SON, the PRINCE, a bit of a CAD,
> Who LOVED the GIRL, so PRETTY but SAD,
> Who DANCED for the MAN, so OLD and BAD,
> Who PAID for the DRINK
> Which SAVED the MOTHER
> Who WEPT to HEAR
> The WIZARD who CURSED
> The CHILDREN who SLEPT
> In the HOUSE that MAN BUILT.

All the words printed in capitals have their appropriate gestures. How many can you work out for yourself?

Mime is not a dead art. It can never die as long as people meet who cannot speak or understand each other's language. We have only to watch the children, or ourselves for that matter, trying to convey something to a friend behind a third person's back. Far from dying, new gestures come into being year after year. What about the thumbs up of 'O.K.', 'just the job', or 'wizard'? (thanks to the R.A.F. the latter has rather altered its meaning since the days of classical ballet). And the hitch-hiking sign, 'going my way?'

There is one last point about mime. We have seen how many of its gestures are the same for more than one word. Of course, most of them are made clear by the context of the mime sequence, just as the difference between 'bough', 'bow', etc., are clear in speaking although they are pronounced the same. In mime a futher distinction can be made by the use of facial expression. It provides the same 'punch' to gesture that vocal inflection does to speech; for instance, Marshall Hall, the famous K.C., once secured an acquittal on a charge of murder, by basing his case on the way in which the accused had cried: 'Speak, speak, speak.'

If you think that much of this mime business is mere hair-splitting and all too erudite and difficult, just think of Harpo Marx. He never speaks a word, but is one ever at a loss to know what he means? That's mime.

MIME DIALOGUES

1. The Curse of CARABOSSE and the Reply of the LILAC FAIRY, from *The Sleeping Princess*, Act I.

CARABOSSE: You—me—forget—why—you—hear—me—speak.
(*Why did you forget me? Listen to what I say.*)
She—grows—she—grows—beautiful—lovely arms.
(*That baby will grow up to be very beautiful with lovely arms.*)
But—she—grows—she—pricks finger—she—dies.
(*But when she is grown up, she will prick her finger and die.*)

(Much triumphant wicked laughter. This piece is very much a character mime and is spread over a lot of music.)

LILAC FAIRY: I cry your mercy—I cry your mercy.
(*Excuse my interrupting, accept my apologies.*)
I—love—there—you—kill—why.
(*I love the baby over there. Why will you kill her?*)
You—hear—me—speak.
(*Listen to what I say.*)
She—pricks finger—sleeps—dies—not.
(*She will prick her finger and fall asleep; she will not die.*)

37

There—comes—lift up—carry—wait.
(*From over there her people will come to lift her up and carry her away. Wait till I have finished. . . .*)
There—come—handsome man—kiss—brow—save.
(*From there will come a handsome man, who will kiss her on the brow and save her.*)

These sentences are easier to follow if one knows that the stage is set like this:

◇ Baby's cradle

King

X   O   Queen

Carabosse   Lilac Fairy

2. Dialogue between ODETTE, the Swan Queen, and Prince SIEGFRIED, from *Swan Lake*, Act II.

PRINCE: You—fly away—not.
(*Do not fly away.*)

ODETTE: I—you—afraid.
(*I'm afraid of you.*)

PRINCE: Why?

ODETTE: You—me—shoot.
(*You will shoot me.*)

PRINCE: I—you—shoot—never—I—you—protect.
(*I will never shoot you. I will protect you.*)

ODETTE: Thank you.

PRINCE: You—here—why.
(*Why are you here?*)

ODETTE: I—queen—swan.
(*I am the Swan Queen.*)

PRINCE: I—you—salute—you—queen—swan—why.
(*I honour you. Why are you the Swan Queen?*)

ODETTE: Wait—there—lake—my—mother—tears . . .
(*I will tell you. That lake over there was made by my mother's tears.*)
One—magician—me—queen—swan . . .
(*A magician turned me into the Swan Queen.*)
But—if—one—me—love—me—marry . . .
(*But if someone loves and marries me*)
I—save—I—swan—no more.
(*I shall be saved and will no longer be a Swan.*)

38

PRINCE: I—you—love—I—you—marry. . . .
  (*I love you and will marry you.*)
  I—swear—magician—where.
  (*I swear it. Where is this magician?*)

ODETTE: There (*pointing to Rothbart's Corner*)—mercy.
  (*Over there. To Rothbart—Have mercy*)

PRINCE: I—shoot.
  (*I will shoot him.*)

(He is stopped from this rash course by ODETTE, who holds an Arabesque right in the line of fire.)

DICTIONARY OF MIME MOVEMENTS

AFRAID, FEAR, FRIGHTEN. Plate 63. Hide the face with the hands and push away.

ANGER, ANGRY, BAD, MAGICIAN, WIZARD. Shake the clenched fists above the head, elbows forward.

BEAUTIFUL, GIRL, WOMAN (or BEAUTIFUL GIRL, WOMAN). Start as in Plate 64a. Make the movement of outlining the shape of the face with the back of the tip of the middle finger, passing through the positions shown in Plates 64 b and c. The hand turns as it passes the forehead. End as in Plate 64a.

BROW. Lightly touch the centre of the brow with the first finger, back of the hand outwards.

BUILD, BUILT, MAKE. Strike the palm of one hand twice with the clenched fist of the other.

BUT, IF. The position is held as in Plate 80a.

CAD (a modern interpolation). The twiddling of imaginary moustachios.

CARRY. A movement as of picking up a child, one hand coming from each side.

CHILD. Position as in Plate 65a.

CHILDREN, GROW. Plates 65 a, b, and c. These positions done in series, as measuring increasing heights.

COME. Start as in Plate 66a, take two steps forward, changing the arms to position shown in Plate 66b. Finish with three little circles of the hands, representing three small steps.

CRY, TEARS, WEEP. Cover face with hands as in Plate 67a, raise head, drawing hands lightly down face, fingers fluttering, to position as in Plate 67b.

CRY (or BEG) YOUR MERCY. Stretch arms forward to position of Plate 68a, bend forward, and open arms smoothly to position shown in Plate 68b.

CURSE, DIE. Take arms up at the side high above the head. Bring them down firmly to position of Plate 69.

DANCE. Both arms above the head, one hand above the other, a small port de bras circling the hands round each other, open them through the fifth position. A peasant depicts 'dance' by step, hop, once each side, leg raised in front, arms in second position opposite the raised leg.

DIE, CURSE. See CURSE.

DRINK. Movement as though raising a glass and drinking.

EVERYTHING. See SAVE.

FLY AWAY. Both arms wave together, from low position to high, starting on the side nearest the person addressed and ending away from him. Two steps away are usually added.

FORGET, KNOW, REMEMBER. Tip of the first finger of either hand on the temple.

FRIENDS. Hands clasped together as in Plate 70 (right).

FRIGHTENED, AFRAID. See AFRAID.

GIRL. See BEAUTIFUL.

GIVE ALL. See SAVE.

GREET. A courtesy movement of one hand, towards the person greeted, from the shoulder, and with a slight bow of the head.

GROW, CHILDREN. See CHILDREN.

HANDSOME, MAN. Place thumb and middle finger of one hand on either side of forehead (but not touching it). Bring hand straight down face to the point of the chin: closing thumb towards fingers. If the gentleman has a beard, the same movement is repeated as far down as the beard is supposed to be. (Pl. 76)

HE. See SHE.

HEAR. Tap the lobes of the ears twice with the middle finger of each hand.

HERE, OBEY. See Plate 71; a quarter turn of the wrist alters the meaning.

HOUSE. Hands held flat, thumbs together, fingers towards person addressed; then outline the shape of a house—roof, walls, floor.

I. One hand points to diaphragm, middle finger leading the way.

IF, BUT. See BUT.

KILL. Stab yourself with (imaginary) dagger. Plate 72.

KING, QUEEN. See Plates 81 a and b. The hands move straight from the one position to the other, as if outlining a crown.

KISS. First finger touches pursed lips, nail to the front.

KNOW. See FORGET.

LAKE. See Plates 73 a and b. The change from a to b indicates the flat surface of the lake.

LIFT UP. Bend down and pick up an imaginary baby, one hand each side of it.

LISTEN, HEAR. See HEAR.

LOVE. See Plate 74. Both hands touch the heart.

LOVELY ARMS. From the position of Plate 75 move hand down arm to finger-tip; repeat with other arm.

MAD. Tear the hair.

MAN, HANDSOME. See HANDSOME.

MAGICIAN, ANGRY, WICKED, WIZARD. See ANGRY.

MARRY. First finger of right hand points to the wedding-ring finger. Plate 77.

ME. Middle fingers of both hands *together* point to diaphragm (*cf.* 1).

MERCY, PLEASE. Fingers interlaced as in Plate 70 (left). MERCY is a more urgent gesture than PLEASE.

MOTHER. See Plate 78.

NEVER, NO, NONE, NO ONE, NOT. See Plates 79 a, b, c. Each gesture leads into the other, making one complete movement, with a slight shake of the head.

OBEY. Point to the floor, back of the hand outwards. (Pl. 71, left).

OLD. Bowed shoulders, three doddering steps.

ONE. See Plate 80c. Note the difference between other gestures on the same plate. Further numbers are shown by the addition of the remaining fingers; the thumb is never used, therefore after FOUR one starts again with the first finger. Each number must have a separate turn of the wrist (e.g. conversation, Queen-Prince in *Swan Lake*, Act I), and the back of the hand always faces outwards.

PAY. Counting money from one hand into the palm of the other hand.

PERHAPS. See Plate 80b.

PLEASE. See MERCY.

PRETTY. See BEAUTIFUL.

PRICK. Prick the afflicted part with a needle (imaginary); e.g. conversation Carabosse—Lilac Fairy in *The Sleeping Princess*, Act I.

PRINCE, PRINCESS. See Plate 81. Same gesture as KING or QUEEN, but done with one hand only.

PROTECT. See Plate 61. The Prince is saying PROTECT.

QUEEN, KING. See KING.

REMEMBER, FORGET, KNOW. See FORGET.

SAD. Hide face in hands. Plate 67a.

SAVE. A lifting movement by both arms (Plate 82a), palms upwards, ending as in Plate 82b. Also used for EVERYTHING, GIVE ALL.

SEE. Middle finger of *one* hand touches the face under each eye, starting on the opposite side to the hand used.

SHE, HE. Usually simply a pointing gesture towards the person concerned or the place where he or she was last seen.

SLEEP. See Plate 83.

SON. As in Lilac Fairy conversation, when referring to the Baby, SON is indicated by pointing in the direction in which he is supposed to be.

SPEAK. Thumb and third finger of alternate hands move as if bringing words from the mouth (Plates 84 a and b); end as in Plate 84c.

STOP. See WAIT.

SWAN. Arms outstretched to each side with a waving movement as of wings. (Swans are the only birds which appear in classical mime.)

SWEAR, VOW. Left hand on heart, right hand raised, palm forward.

TEARS, WEEP, CRY. See CRY.

THANK YOU. See Plate 61. The Swan Queen is saying THANK YOU. (This can be done less emphatically with one hand only, as in GREET.)

THERE. According to the situation, *either* a broad gesture with the hand open *or* a definite point in the direction indicated.

WAIT, STOP. One hand raised, as when a traffic policeman indicates 'stop'.

WEEP, TEARS, CRY. See CRY.

WHO? HOW? WHAT? WHERE? WHY? See Plates 85 a, b, c, d. These four plates represent one smooth gesture; the exact meaning has to be guessed from the context.

WIZARD, WICKED, ANGRY. See ANGRY.

WOMAN. See BEAUTIFUL.

YOU. Indicating person addressed, with open hand (polite) or with a pointing hand (rude).

Chapter V

THE MECHANICS OF A BALLET

HOW DOES A ballet come to be made? Who and how many people are responsible for that work of art which we call a classical ballet? How is it put together? What makes the classical ballet *tick*?

The first thing to realize is that classical ballets are to-day very rarely seen in their entirety. Nowadays, an evening's entertainment is made up of three or four ballets, of which excerpts from the 'classics' form only part of the programme. There are exceptions, such as the Sadler's Wells *Sleeping Princess* and *Swan Lake*, and some ballets presented by the International Ballet Company; but for the most part to-day we see only one act of a classical ballet, or just the most exciting divertissements. Yet, when they were first presented, these same classics lasted the whole evening, through three or four acts.

Swan Lake is a typical example. The original four-act ballet lasts some three hours. But Act II can stand on its own, it is complete in story and dancing without any of the others, and it is the Act II of *Swan Lake* which we see most often to-day. Very frequently, it provides the classic element in an evening's ballet. If we try to take this Act II to pieces, we may discover a little of what to look for in other ballets.

Swan Lake comes to us from Russia. Ballet reached Russia through the French ballet masters, took root there, and grew into a national art of great vigour and beauty, at a time when it was going through a very bad patch in France. Towards the end of the nineteenth century all ballets in Russia were designed within a well-defined form. Whatever the story, there had to be various styles of dances, from character dances to technical dances, for various numbers of artists, from the full company down to dances for six, five, four, three, two, and one so that every kind of talent had a chance to show itself, from the corps de ballet (sometimes numbering over fifty) to the ballerina and her cavalier. The mime sequences came between the dances; they told the story, gave the dancers a chance to act, and afforded them a necessary physical rest. Such a framework guaranteed the gradual development of an artist, and the highly critical audiences of that day took great delight in watching their favourites improve, much as to-day one watches the progress of a promising filly or a rising young boxer. This audience was well qualified to spot the abilities of the dancers, as well as to criticize the merits of the music and décor of each ballet; in fact it was an audience of connoisseurs, which accounts for the strict conventions in the ballet of that day. It was not until 1909, with the advent of the Russian Ballet of Diaghileff, that the rest of Europe learnt what had been going on in Russia all this time; but for Diaghileff, we in this country might never have seen what we call 'our' classical ballets.

Swan Lake was first produced at the Maryinsky Theatre, St Petersburg in 1895. Tchaikovsky, the leading ballet composer of his day, was asked to write music which would illustrate the story as exactly as possible. The plot, with all its details and various divertissements, was spread over four acts.

It is not known who was the original designer of sets and costumes for *Swan Lake*, but Plate 87 shows one of the earliest designs for Act II, which is set by a lake in the moonlight. The décor is the only part of a ballet which can change through the years. Different designers can try their hands at new settings which they think are the most attractive for a ballet, and there have been many changes of set and costumes for *Swan Lake*; but the music and choreography (the arrangement of the dances) must never be altered, otherwise it becomes a different ballet on the same subject. Unfortunately, details of the steps are sometimes altered by time. (See p. 60.) The dancing and the music are inextricably allied; clearly one cannot fit the same groups of steps to two quite different pieces of music.

Which brings us to that most important person, the choreographer. He (or she) makes the ballet itself, works out all the steps and arm movements of every dancer on the stage, arranges their exits and entrances, thinks out the patterns of the dances, how to fit them in with the phrases of the music and how to put the story over with the greatest dramatic effect. The choreographers for *Swan Lake* were Pétipa and his assistant Lev Ivanov. Pétipa was a Frenchman who accepted an engagement in St Petersburg and stayed there for the rest of his life; he became known as the 'father of the ballet', because most of the great ballets of that day were his, and he set the style of such productions as *Swan Lake* and *Sleeping Princess*, which are now known as classics. It is hard to judge to-day how much of *Swan Lake* was created by Pétipa and how much by his assistant, but Act II is generally attributed to Ivanov.

The story of *Swan Lake*, Act II concerns Prince Siegfried, who is hunting swans by night with his friends. They sight a large flight of them (I believe the correct hunting term is a herd), but as the Prince is about to shoot the leading swan he sees that it is a beautiful woman wearing a crown. She tells the Prince that she and her companions are all enchanted maidens, who can assume human form only between midnight and dawn. Siegfried falls in love with the Swan Queen and vows to marry her, so as to break the enchantment with his love; but as dawn approaches, she and her maids-in-waiting become swans again, gliding away across the lake. The power of the Magicain who has enchanted them defeats all attempts to follow her, and Siegfried is left desolate.

The original cast for Act II calls for the Swan Queen (Odette), Prince Siegfried, his friend Benno, Rothbart the Magician, sixteen Huntsmen and some forty Swan Maidens. Few companies can afford this number nowadays, and so the numbers of Huntsmen and Maidens are reduced, while Rothbart frequently becomes merely a green light or a sinister shadow. Although the classical ballets were planned on the grand scale, it is quite possible to reduce them in size; so, whether they are performed by thirty-two, sixteen, or sometimes even fewer dancers, the steps and patterns remain the same, with the stage patterns just a size or two smaller.

Act II lasts twenty-five minutes and is divided into ten sections, ten different dances or scenes, expertly arranged to contrast with each other in length and in character, yet each one balancing those on either side of it; the whole builds up into a ballet which can stand on its own, even though it is but one of four acts. In no ballet is this controlled contrast within a set framework seen to better advantage.

There are three things to consider when examining the dancing. First, an important point in any ballet, the pattern that the dancers make on the floor; second, the steps used in the dances themselves; and third, the work of the Swan Queen herself as the central figure in the act (the Prince's role in Act II is entirely that of Cavalier).

There is one important point to remember about 'pattern'. A ballet is never designed to be seen from only one spot; the choreographer must always remember that his work will be seen simultaneously from stalls, circle, and gallery. Now, each of these viewpoints gives a completely different picture of the stage, so the dances must look good not only from straight in front (stalls), but also from a high angle (gallery), and from an angle of 45° (circle). The pattern must be pleasing both horizontally and vertically, as it were; if you go to the same ballet more than once, it is a good idea to see it from different parts of the auditorium. Moreover, 'pattern' includes the designs made by the dancers' bodies in lifts, arabesques, and so on, not just the design traced upon the floor. In addition to floor pattern, therefore, the choreographer must think of his 'air pattern' as well.

Swan Lake is romantic in theme, and so the choreographers' problem was to devise steps which would be beautiful to look at and at the same time would remind the audience that they were supposed to be watching a herd of swans with human souls. The actual steps in *Swan Lake* are comparatively simple—there are few that have not been dealt with in Chapter I. But all of them, combined with arm and body movements, are put together to indicate the behaviour of swans—frightened swans, peaceful swans, happy swans, very young swans, or flying swans, but always swans.

It is this which makes the role of Odette, the Swan Queen, so difficult. She cannot capture the audience with an immediate display of technical brilliance, as her rival, Odile the Magician's Daughter, can do in the next Act. Odette's entrance in Act II is her first appearance in the ballet and from the start she must convince everybody that she is half-swan, half-girl; that she is a Princess; that she is humanly in love with Siegfried; of her hope of salvation in his love; and of her ever-present fear of the magician. This is not easy to do in arabesques and bourrées, and it explains why sometimes a performance which is technically faultless nevertheless leaves one cold. Odette must be an actress as well as a dancer.

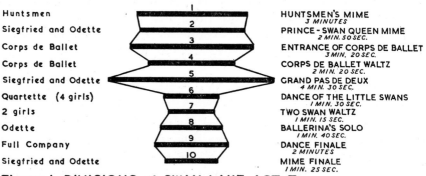

Huntsmen	1	HUNTSMEN'S MIME *3 MINUTES*
Siegfried and Odette	2	PRINCE - SWAN QUEEN MIME *2 MIN. 50 SEC.*
Corps de Ballet	3	ENTRANCE OF CORPS DE BALLET *3 MIN. 20 SEC.*
Corps de Ballet	4	CORPS DE BALLET WALTZ *2 MIN. 20 SEC.*
Siegfried and Odette	5	GRAND PAS DE DEUX *4 MIN. 30 SEC.*
Quartette (4 girls)	6	DANCE OF THE LITTLE SWANS *1 MIN. 30 SEC.*
2 girls	7	TWO SWAN WALTZ *1 MIN. 15 SEC.*
Odette	8	BALLERINA'S SOLO *1 MIN. 40 SEC.*
Full Company	9	DANCE FINALE *2 MINUTES*
Siegfried and Odette	10	MIME FINALE *1 MIN. 25 SEC.*

Figure I. DIVISIONS of SWAN LAKE ACT II

Figure I is a graph of this act, showing the ten divisions into scenes or dances, and their respective lengths; it also shows the characters mainly concerned in each section. Let's take Act II to pieces, division by division, and see what it has to show us.

(1) *The Huntsman's Mime* (3 minutes). This is merely a preparation for what is to come, in the same way as a playwright usually begins his second act with some unimportant detail in order to let everyone get back to their seats. There is no obvious pattern, since it is mime only. The huntsmen 'plant' a portion of the plot—they are out to shoot swans, swans are expected in the neighbourhood, they are looking for swans. This, incidentally, is surprisingly difficult to convey with any show of conviction. Then the swans are sighted, and the Prince, rather snobbishly, desires to be left alone while he takes first shot. The huntsmen exit and the Prince, as he watches the swans fly nearer, suddenly realizes that the leader wears a crown and that she has changed, or is changing, into a woman. He hides off stage to watch this mystery.

(2) *Prince—Swan Queen Mime* (2 minutes, 50 seconds). The stage has been cleared for the first entrance of the ballerina, a great moment in any classical ballet; remember that this is the first time that we, or that earlier audience who saw all four acts, have seen her. The Swan Queen enters, a glistening, white, dramatic figure on the empty stage, the solitary, enchanted Princess, not yet quite free of her spell, still half bird and half woman. She appears from a part of the stage which can only be described as Rothbart's Corner (upstage right, as seen from the audience); all the swans, including Odette, enter here, as if temporarily released from the Magician's influence; they exit the same way when the spell takes effect again, and it is here that Rothbart makes his sinister appearance. The effect is one of magnetic evil, as if the magician were so powerful that he doesn't need to move about, but merely draws his victims back into his circle at will.

The step with which Odette makes her first appearance is as near to a swan alighting as classical ballet can make it. It is followed by slow arabesques, and a beautiful preening head movement, until the moment when she is surprised by the Prince. He still carries his crossbow in his hand, so her terror is natural enough. The ensuing mime scene between them, as they meet for the first time, is interspersed with dancing, and so has a pattern (Fig. IIa, page 50). On first sighting the Prince, she wings away from him across the stage and he follows her; they have a mime conversation, and then Odette describes a wide circle of arabesques, as though making up her mind about Siegfried, finally returning to him to answer his mime questions. She tells him her story. (The details of this mime colloquy are given on p. 38.)

Then they go off, walking quietly together in mutual trust—*not* through Rothbart's Corner, because she is now a princess and under Siegfried's spell rather than the wizard's.

The whole section is like the first chapter of a novel, setting the scene for coming events.

(3) *Entrance of the Corps de Ballet* (3 minutes, 20 seconds). Now it is time for the dancing proper to start. It is the first time we have seen the Swan Maidens, so they enter from Rothbart's Corner as if flying out from under his enchantment. Figure IIb shows the main floor pattern of this dance. Just as every piece of music is written in a certain key, so every dance has its characteristic pattern, and this one is composed of curves and circles. The steps are few, and there is one arm movement of which a lot of use is made, a slow beat of the arms, just like that of a swan's wings; this and the circling patterns give the impression of swans. At one point, the corps de ballet form an arrowhead group, the shape of a group of swans in flight, and it is thus that Benno discovers them. Before he can call his companions, he is surrounded by circling swans.

The step used for the Swan Maidens' entrance is a *temp levé*, in arabesque, and then four petits jetés, repeated very often; simple enough in itself, but when combined with the décor, the lighting, and the music, the pattern in which it is danced, and the number of dancers, one does not ask for more. Yet, it is sufficiently different in feeling to set the Swan Queen apart from her maidens.

At the end of the dance, Benno calls the huntsmen to him, and they prepare to shoot. The 'swans'—presumably, they have not yet completely turned into girls or the men would hardly want to shoot them —gather in a close group, with the hunters opposite. The situation is saved by the dramatic return of the Prince, followed by Odette. She enters on a wide curve, which brings her to rest between her maidens and the crossbows of the men. She prays Siegfried to forbid them to shoot; Siegfried dismisses his puzzled followers, who disperse into the forest, followed by Odette and her lover. This short passage serves to keep the two principals in the forefront of the audience's mind, to whet their appetite for the beauty of the approaching pas-de-deux and to break up the formal series of dances. It also preserves the continuity of the story and the mood.

(4) *The Swan Waltz* (2 minutes, 20 seconds). The stage is now occupied only by the Swan Maidens, and they dance their waltz as though in relief at their recent escape. In contrast with their first entrance, the floor pattern is all straight lines (Fig. IIc, page 50) up, down and across the stage. This not only makes an effective change from the previous circular pattern but also accentuates the human side of the maidens (momentarily free of their spell), as opposed to their swan existence. As variations on the main theme of straight lines, pairs of girls circle round each other during the dance, but this does not disturb the key line of the waltz any more than grace notes alter the key of a piece of music.

The finish is unexpectedly quiet, in two long lines on each side of the stage; there is a repetition of the bird-like preening movement (translated into a port-de-bras), before they stand quiet and still. There is a delicate avoidance here of a finish which might attract applause and so break the mood for what is to come.

(5) *The Grand Pas-de-Deux* (4½ minutes). Both emotionally and in point of time, the audience is now ready for the centre piece of the Act, and Tchaikovsky warns us what to expect in a very beautiful introduction, during which the Prince enters, followed by Benno, in quest of the Swan Queen. They search for her in vain down the lines of Swan Maidens. Then the ripple of the harp, the perfect music for her entrance, indicates unmistakably that she is near at hand. As if once more struggling against Rothbart, she enters again from the dreaded Corner, poises for a second behind Benno, and then forlornly circles the stage, to

63. AFRAID, FEAR, FRIGHTENED

 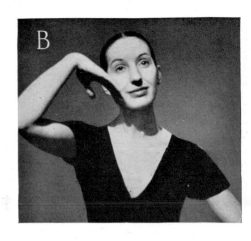

65. A CHILD. If it is followed by B
and C, as though measuring height, it
becomes CHILDREN, or GROW

64. BEAUTIFUL or WOMAN (or both). The middle finger traces the shape of the face

66. COME. B ends with three little circles of the hands, impossible to photograph

67. A, B, CRY, TEARS, WEEP

68. CRY (or BEG) YOUR MERCY. These two positions join together smoothly

69. CURSE, DIE

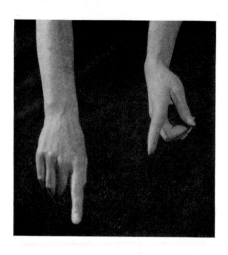

70. Left, PLEASE; MERCY; right, FRIENDS

71. Left, OBEY; right, HERE

72. KILL, with a dagger

73. LAKE. The two positions
make one smooth gesture

74. LOVE

75. LOVELY ARMS. The action
of stroking the arm with the
other hand

B

76. MAN or HANDSOME MAN

77. MARRY

78. MOTHER

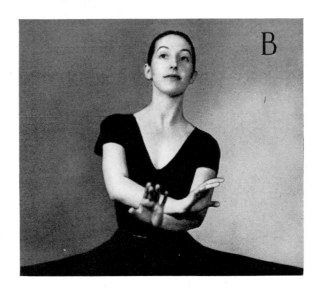

79. NEVER, NO, NONE, NO ONE, NOT. The crossing of the hands is usually done twice, with a shake of the head, thus: A, B, C, B, C, A

80. A, BUT or IF; B, PER-
HAPS; C, ONE (numeral)

C

A

B

A

81. QUEEN, or KING

B

82. SAVE, OR SAVED

83. SLEEP

84. SPEAK

85. WHO? HOW? WHAT? WHERE? WHY? These
four stages are smoothed into one wide gesture

86. Domini Callaghan and David Paltenghi in Act II of *Swan Lake*

88. Domini Callaghan and Michel de Lutry in *The Blue Bird*. B shows the final lift

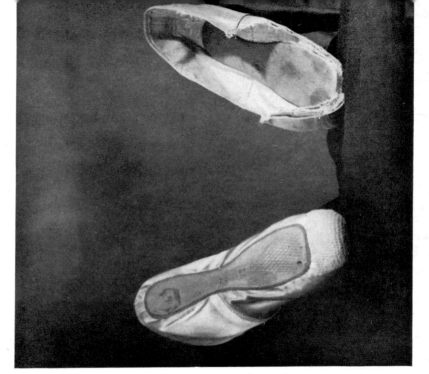

89. Left, the darning on the toe of a point shoe; right, the block itself cut in h

sink at last at the Prince's feet. With the commencement of the melody, the Grand Pas-de-Deux begins.

The long, slow melody and the smoothness of movement both indicate that this is the big moment of the act. The corps de ballet move into groups and then remain still, so that there is no distraction from the two principals; only when they pause for a moment, do the Maidens take over (you will find that the music changes, too) and the girls group and regroup themselves to augment the dance lines of the ballerina and her partner—straight lines to begin with when Odette and Siegfried come straight down the centre, diagonals as they dance on a diagonal, and so on. The floor pattern of the Grand Pas-de-Deux is not so interesting as that of the ensemble dances; the Pas-de-Deux gains its effects mainly by the patterns that the dancers make in the air round about them with the lines of their bodies. Indeed, they need hardly move from one spot, yet the beautiful designs made by their arms and legs leave the audience quite satisfied. All the movements are highly interpretative. Odette glides with the music as a swan glides over the water; although she is for the moment human and in love with Siegfried, she cannot forget the danger which overshadows them nor the form to which she must return: there is the thought of her swan-fate behind her every move. Other emotions are expressed in her dancing—all of it, remember, kept within the conventions of classical ballet. The *Developé* (slow stretching of the leg) and Fall, away from Siegfried into the arms of Benno, enables the audience to realize her ache for the certainty of happiness and her despair at the certainty of her plight. The Prince's devotion revives her courage, and they go into a series of lifts, as if she were full of hope for the future but, knowing their mutual danger, she tries to leave him. When the proper emotional contact between dancers and audience is established, the everyday mechanics of these lifts become transformed; Siegfried is no longer setting his partner down upon the stage but seems to be gently and lovingly restraining her from taking flight. Now and again she makes a pathetic appeal towards the menace of Rothbart's Corner. The highly technical finish of the pas-de-deux, with its quivering *petits battements* on the ankle and its *finger fouetté* pirouettes is not out of place in such a situation, any more than is a difficult and beautiful aria sung by an operatic soprano who is supposed to be at the point of death. Both are conventions accepted in their own sphere. The final slow stretch of the leg in the 2nd Position, ending with a fall into the arms of Benno, is a perfectly legitimate way for the classical ballet to convey a heart torn between love and fear.

And convey it it does, *if* the ballerina is an actress as well as a dancer. It is not until one sees the steps as they would be done in the classroom and then compares them with the finished performance on the stage that one realizes just how much 'interpretation' means in ballet—all the difference between reading Shakespeare for the first time at school and seeing his work brought to life by an Olivier or a Gielgud.

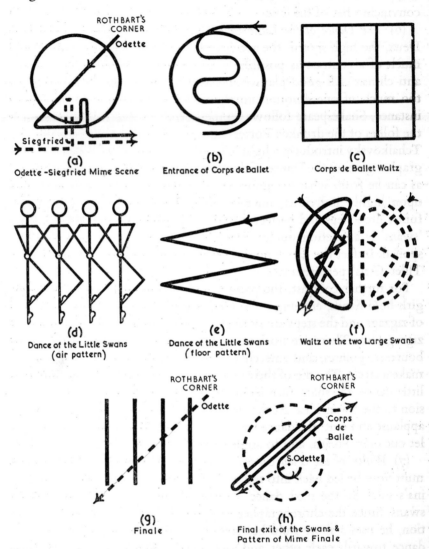

(a)
Odette - Siegfried Mime Scene

(b)
Entrance of Corps de Ballet

(c)
Corps de Ballet Waltz

(d)
Dance of the Little Swans
(air pattern)

(e)
Dance of the Little Swans
(floor pattern)

(f)
Waltz of the two Large Swans

(g)
Finale

(h)
Final exit of the Swans &
Pattern of Mime Finale

NOTE: These diagrams are not intended to show the complete design of the dances, but merely to give the key-patterns round which they are built.

Figure II   Patterns of Swan Lake Act II

Siegfried's part in the Pas-de-Deux is a fine example of the duties of a Cavalier, showing his partner off, supporting her, always in devoted attendance. The very fact that he has no solo stresses the atmosphere of the Act; he is deeply in love, in him there is little of that fear of the future that there is in her, until the closing moments of the act he does not realize the awful implications of Rothbart's spell, he is confident of himself, and his whole being is concentrated upon protecting Odette and convincing her of his love.

(6) *The Dance of the Little Swans* (1½ minutes). The Grand Pas-de-Deux, the high spot of the act, is over. Something entirely different, as much of a contrast as possible, is now needed to prevent a feeling of anti-climax. All good playwrights know that an audience cannot take too much of one emotion unrelieved—which is why in *Macbeth*, for instance, Shakespeare follows up the horrors of Duncan's murder with the follies of the drunken Porter—and it is the same with ballet. So now Tchaikovsky introduces a light, cheeky passage of music and the choreographer gives us the Dance of the Little Swans. This is as sharply different as can be from what has gone before. Instead of gliding dignity based upon highly individual interpretation, we have quick, light, almost funny little steps and perfect precision. If one of the quartette of young 'swans' is a fraction out of time with the others, the whole effect is spoiled. In fact the dance might almost have been the forerunner of the Tiller Girls' performances.

For further contrast, the pattern is zigzag (Fig. IId and e). The four girls hold hands, crossing each other's arms. The floor pattern is a series of zigzags and the steps are swift and sharp, which makes the legs appear zigzag also. There are no long lines anywhere, all small jetés, pas-de-bourrées, pointes, and entrechats, and the dancers never turn round or make a circle. The use of their heads is a notable feature of this attractive little dance, the sharp turning and slow bending being the only concession to the Swan idea. At the end of the dance, all the girls take their applause and exit; the dance has given the audience a chance to relax, to let out their breath, and to smile a little.

(7) *Waltz of the Two Swans* (1 minute, 15 seconds). The audience must now be led back into the original mood, to prepare for the ballerina's solo. So the next dance, another waltz, is given to two 'senior' swans. Since the choreographer is aiming not at contrast but at transition, he uses a more fluid but still zigzag floor pattern. The two girls dance towards each other and away again, finally circling their own halves of the stage and starting all over again (Fig. II), the complete floor pattern being, in fact, kidney shaped. However, the steps, arm movements, and 'air pattern' return to the previous flowing style. The steps are again very simple, but they are broader and heavier than anything else in the ballet. It is an exhausting dance to do and, on the whole, unrewarding.

In this dance, and the little pas-de-quatre before it, the balletomanes of old would look for the first budding talent among the junior members of the company.

(8) *The Ballerina's Solo* (1 minute, 40 seconds). Again the stage is left empty for the Swan Queen's entrance and again, as in the Pas-de-Deux, it is air pattern rather than floor pattern which counts. As before, her steps are simple enough when seen in the classroom—for example, sissone-sissone-pas de bourée-arabesque—but the lines of arms, body, and head, and the way the simple steps are phrased to the music take it very far from the classroom. Though it looks simple, it is a solo one can work at endlessly, never tiring of it, never exhausting the possibilities of interpretation. The reward of such endless labour comes when seasoned audiences are left breathless and believing at the sight of it.

(9) *Dance Finale* (2 minutes). The finale is danced by the full company, as convention demands. The key pattern is once more one of straight lines. It begins with the dancers coming down the stage, from backcloth to footlights, four at a time; each four separates, two moving to either side. The centre of the stage is always occupied by four dancers coming forward. This figure ends in two long lines on each side of the stage. The steps of this section are intriguing because those used when coming down the stage have a downward accent, while those used as the girls travel back again have an upward accent, and the two accents are kept going against each other. There follows an exciting entrance for the Swan Queen, when she travels in a long diagonal right across the stage, in sharp contrast to the straight lines of the corps de ballet on each side; her arms and legs, too, make diagonal air patterns, either straight in front of her or straight behind her in arabesque. (Fig. IIg gives the key pattern.) Last comes a quick, brilliant, and very short bit of footwork, leading into the build-up for the final tableau when Benno and the Prince come on just in time to join the picture. The tableau leaves plenty of opportunity for applause and yet one is left with the feeling that something more is to follow—Benno and Siegfried can hardly have made that sudden entrance just to provide a striking pose for the ballerina. Sure enough, there is a sad Mime sequence still to come.

Mime Finale (1 minute, 25 seconds). Dawn breaks and, as the Prince sets Odette on the ground (Pl. 86), she realizes that she must leave him. She waves her maidens back to the lake and the final pattern they make is a sad, slow circle which takes them back to Rothbart's Corner and out of sight (Fig. IIh, page 50). The smooth run and slow, beating motion of the arms, as in their first appearance, shows that they are returning to their swan shapes. When she follows them, Odette, too, reverses the pattern of her first entrance and the final arabesque, when she flies back from the very shadow of Rothbart for a last farewell, is very moving.

This last scene contains only bourrées and arabesques. The reversal of the opening patterns by both Odette and her maidens is very important, for it rounds off the pattern of the whole act; the little scene leads gently away from the excitement of the Finale and balances with the quiet mime sequence which opened the act. It also reminds us once again of the swan-spell and stresses Rothbart's evil strength, so that when Siegfried rushes after his love we take it for granted that the Magician's mere presence (actual or implied) will prevent him from following her, and there is nothing incongruous in his despairing collapse as the curtain falls.

So much for the plot and mechanics of *Swan Lake*, Act II. The rigid conventions at this stage of any classical ballet have been faithfully observed—a solo for the ballerina (the male dancer gets his solo in the next act, in which Odette appears only as a vision), a Grand pas-de-deux, some mime to establish the plot, a dance for two budding soloists, a dance for the more promising youngsters, dances for the corps de ballet and a finale for the full company. Yet these conventions have been subtly used so as to produce the maximum emotional impact. The order in which they are presented stimulates the reactions of the audience in a way which might be the envy of any psychologist, but never allows us to forget the atmosphere of the story. So too, the simple classroom steps of ballet have been put together to invoke, with the aid of beautiful music and good dancers, the moon-haunted, magical atmosphere of maidens who are half swans, and of undying devotion.

Lastly, a word about the environment of classical ballet, the world *in* which and *for* which *Coppélia*, *Swan Lake*, and the *Sleeping Princess*, were created. That world, which produced and accepted those strict conventions for its ballets, would perhaps seem rather hidebound to us to-day.

The home from which these ballets emigrated was Theatre Street in St Petersburg. Theatre Street was a cul-de-sac, an aloof little world of its own, dedicated to the Art of Ballet. From the day when the students entered the school at the age of nine, until some six years later when they graduated on the stage of the Maryinsky Theatre, they never left Theatre Street, save for a visit to their families two or three times a year. The discipline was convent-like. No student was allowed to go to parties in the outside world; boys and girls met only at rehearsals, never in ordinary school or dancing classes. Many of them never left Theatre Street until they retired with a pension. The Ballet was their whole life.

The audience was rather like the most exclusive type of club. The mere fact that you had enough money to pay for it did not ensure a seat at the Maryinsky; you had to file a petition with the Chancery of the

Imperial Theatres and, once a seat was allotted, it was handed down from father to son. Consequently, enormous pleasure, interest, and prejudice grew up around every performance. The audience knew every step of past ballets and criticized every step of the new ones; they knew every member of the company by name and had followed every single one of their performances from their first appearances as nervous students; they assembled at the theatre knowing exactly who had danced well at the last performance, who had been 'off balance', and just where they had gone wrong, wondering how the junior soloists were shaping, or if a previously-noted youngster would to-night come up to expectation. In the intervals, furiously sincere arguments would develop between hereditary neighbours in the stalls over the rival merits of, say, the talented young Tamara Karsavina and the promising little Anna Pavlova.

In fact, in those days it was almost as difficult and quite as much an honour for the laity to become a member of the Maryinsky audience as it was for a dancer to become a member of the company. This bred an understanding, a sense of mutual achievement, almost a family feeling between dancers and audience which has never been recaptured, although a faint reflection of it could be seen in the early days of the Old Vic and the Sadler's Wells. The worlds from which their audiences came could not have been further apart but perhaps the spirit was the same.

It was in this atmosphere that the great names of ballet grew up and graduated—Kchessinska, Preoprajenskaya, Spessivtzeva, Karsavina, Pavlova, Nijinsky. The best picture of that life is to be found in *Theatre Street*, the fascinating autobiography of Mme Karsavina, who now lives in London. Although one may have a lot to say against the closed shop and monastic existence of that world, it had one definite advantage over the ballet life of to-day. The graded training and lengthy apprenticeship made sure that no dancer assumed a solo role until he or she was physically equal to it. This gave every dancer a far longer maturity than is the case to-day, when the pressure of modern conditions all too frequently makes a pipe-dream of the gradual development of both technique and artistry. How often does one see some 'baby ballerina', full of infinite promise, overburdened with important roles before she is ready for them, with the result that she quite literally 'wears out' physically before reaching her artistic maturity.

As for the audience, next time you go to see *Swan Lake*, even if it is only Act II, settle yourself comfortably during the overture and imagine yourself in your seat at the Maryinsky Theatre, your own hereditary seat held by your father before you, studying the richly elaborate programme, polishing your opera-glasses, bowing to your friends, and noticing which of the Royal Family is present to-night. This is quite easy to do in Convent Garden, but in even the meanest theatre it will help to take your mind off ration queues and Class Z Reserve, which is surely one of the main functions of the classical ballet these days.

Chapter VI

BALLET WORKSHOP

THERE ARE MANY things which are a necessary part of a ballet, but which have nothing to do with the actual technique of dancing. Many craftsmen contribute to the finished work of art.

Not the least important is the point shoe. In Chapter I, I mentioned the special stiffening on the instep and the thin papier maché toeblock of the modern ballet shoe. Plate 89b shows how the papier maché graduates away from the tip of the toe into the satin.

Point shoes have altered a lot since they were first invented about a hundred years ago. They have become progressively stronger, heavier, and harder, as more and more pointwork was demanded in ballets. Originally, pointwork was done with no blocking at all in the shoes. During her brilliant career, so much of which was passed at the Empire Theatre, Dame Adeline Genée refused the assistance offered by the new-fangled stiffened shoe, with the result that her silent lightness of elevation and the speed of her pointwork are still famous. That is proof that point shoes are only meant to be a help to strong feet and not in themselves a means to an end. Although one can jump, hop, and run on point for miles in our modern shoes, I am not altogether convinced that they are an advantage. It's not easy to be a Sylphide or a Swan when one's shoes 'clonk' every time one jumps; and young dancers are dangerously apt to rely more on their shoes than on the strength of their own feet. Perhaps, in these days of plastics, someone will invent a ballet shoe which combines the best aspects of both old and new shoes.

The papier maché in the tip of the shoe becomes soft and wears out very quickly. Most dancers, therefore, darn the tips of their 'points' with heavy embroidery thread (Pl. 89a), which gives the shoe a slightly longer life and helps to deaden the sound of landing on a hard stage. An alternative method is to cover the points with glue.

The shoe ribbons are lined with tape to within about four inches of the ends so that, should the ribbon break, the tapes will hold. When sewing on the ribbons, the dancer folds over the heel of the shoe and stitches them to the angle of the material (Pl. 90a). If the ribbons are wrongly placed they can restrict the instep or ankle. When the shoe is put on, the heel of the tights is damped with a little homely spit, followed by rosin, to make sure it will not slip off; men sometimes go so far as to use seccotine on their soft shoes. Plate 90b shows how point shoes should be tied. The ribbons are passed across the top of the foot, round the back of the leg and to the front again one on top of the other and finished off with a neat bow at the back; the ribbon on the inside of the foot is always underneath, and the ends of the bow must be securely tucked out of sight in the little hollow beside the Achilles tendon. More spit and rosin make sure that the ends do not slip out. There are still companies which levy a small fine for any ribbon end seen during a performance.

Point shoes are never thrown away. They have a brief period of glory, on an average about four days, when they are used on the stage. Then they are relegated to rehearsals, and finally to the classroom, where they are used until one day they quite literally drop off.

Next come 'tights'. Whether they are cotton, silk, or fishnet, they must *never* wrinkle at the knees. To prevent that, each dancer has his or her own favourite system of ropes and pulleys made of tape, elastic, and pennies, but, most important of all, the tights are washed after each performance. 'Cab-horse knees' are guaranteed to ruin the glamour of any ballerina in one fell wrinkle.

A dancer's hair is another worry. It takes a lot of skill to get it firm enough for dancing and yet keep it attractive. Of course, the problem varies considerably. Some hair won't stay up when it is freshly washed, some won't lie down; but the dancer must pirouette and leap and still has no excuse if her hair comes down or if she loses her headdress. One dodge which is frequently used to obtain the classic hair-do is to take a piece of tape about one inch wide and the same colour as the hair—it must be tape, because ribbon slips—and tie it tightly round the head, just above the hair-line in front and underneath the hair at the back. This does not show on the stage and provides a very firm base to which to pin the hair; but the dancer must remember to paint in the hair parting with grease paint. The tape band is also a safe anchorage for head-dresses. Crêpe hair can be used quite safely with such a base to pin it to. Of course, every dancer uses a hair-net with elastic as well.

A dancer must be neat and tidy, from the last hair to the shoe ribbons. Once on the stage, the smallest thing amiss will distract the audience, and there is no time to worry about personal appearance.

The short classical ballet dress, known as a *tutu*, is of immense importance to a performance. A good one makes a ballerina look and feel one hundred per cent better, and it at once brings the element of Fairy Tale on to the stage. It is not merely a pretty costume of conventional shape, it acts as a kind of corset. The waist must fit as tightly as possible so that the bodice will not shift during lifts or supported pirouettes, but over the ribs it must be more free, in order to leave room to bend and breathe. The skirt stands out flat from the hips and graduates in gently

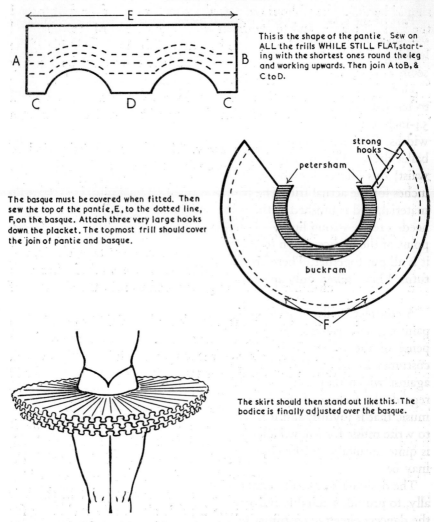

This is the shape of the pantie. Sew on ALL the frills WHILE STILL FLAT, starting with the shortest ones round the leg and working upwards. Then join A to B, & C to D.

The basque must be covered when fitted. Then sew the top of the pantie, E, to the dotted line, F, on the basque. Attach three very large hooks down the placket. The topmost frill should cover the join of pantie and basque.

The skirt should then stand out like this. The bodice is finally adjusted over the basque.

Figure III Making a Tutu

to the top of the thigh; this effect is obtained not by hundreds of frills but by the right kind of frill. The panties are made in one with the basque, and there is no gap between the pantie frills and the skirt frills; they graduate quite evenly from the shortest frills on the edge of the pantie to the longest frills on the top of the skirt. A tutu should be kept either in a hat box large enough not to crush the frills, or hung up by the crutch and covered with cellophane or muslin. The one thing a tutu must never have is that sad lampshade look and the quickest way to develop this is to hang it up by the shoulder straps under a heavy sheet or to wrap it up in a brown paper parcel tied round the middle with string.

Part of the art of a cavalier is to partner a ballerina without damaging her tutu; some cavaliers finish a ballet with their ballerina's costume looking as if it had never been touched, while others manage to make it seem as if it was fresh from the mangle.

Here are some practical notes on the making of a tutu. There are eight to ten frills in the tutu skirt. The top frill takes about twelve widths of 54-inch net. Each descending frill has one width less, down to six widths. (The same theory applies to the four or five skirts in the long ballet dress.) The average length of a tutu skirt is 14 inches from the waist; this allows for about 4 inches down the basque and about 10 inches for the actual frill. The basque is made of buckram, covered with material, and is finished at the waist with strong petersham. The bodice needs a really strong lining—bones are often used, especially to keep the point of the bodice down to the basque. Figure III gives an idea of how it is all put together. There are many tricks of the trade used in making tutus. I have given only an outline of the general method.

A complete ballet as seen on the stage is a partnership between music, painting, and dancing. No one section should obtrude itself at the expense of the others. It is useless if the designer produces wonderful costumes in which the dancers can't move, or a magnificent setting against which they can't be seen; it is useless if the choreographer disregards the feeling of the music and insists on putting a tragic story to music that is joyous; and it is useless if a composer who has been asked to write music for a new ballet insists upon composing something which is quite unsuitable to the choreographer's theme, beautiful as the music may be.

The designer's task is to enhance the atmosphere of the ballet pictorially, to provide a suitable and artistic setting for the dancing, and to give the dancers effective costumes *in which they can dance*. In classical ballets a designer is largely restricted to the tutu or the long ballet frock, to which he can add only colour, texture of material, and decoration. As a further limitation, he must remember the difficulties of partner work; a high headdress would be, in the words of Stanley Holloway, 'knocked skew-wiff' very early in a pas-de-deux; a romantic-seeming scarf might strangle one or both dancers; glittering decorations at the waist could leave the cavalier with bleeding hands. Always the body line of the dancers must be left as clear as possible. Considering all these limitations, the variety of designs which one sees is truly remarkable.

As for the music, the ideal situation is to have it specially commissioned, so that the composer and choreographer can work together from scratch, discussing how much music is needed for each scene, just where the climaxes should come, and how best to bring out the character and atmosphere in sound as well as in vision. The composer can then be sure that his music will not be tampered with and the choreographer knows that he won't have to alter his story to fit a piece of music that is almost, but not quite, right. That 'not quite' has spoiled many a promising ballet.

Of course, a ballet can be fitted very successfully to music already written. Often a choreographer finds an idea growing out of music that he has heard, and that music leads his imagination on until the story is complete. At other times, he gets the idea first and then has to search for music to fit it. This can be a very ticklish job indeed, because if a piece of music stands alone as a work of art in its own right it is nothing but impertinence to try to dance to it, unless you deeply respect the composer's original intentions concerning tempo and feeling. If a choreographer has thought up a delightful series of steps and then finds that they won't fit in to the music which he has chosen, that is his fault, not the composer's; and it is quite wrong to play the music much faster or much slower to suit his own convenience.

Very often a choreographer collects several short pieces by one composer, because they are easily adapted to his idea. If the composer is dead, the choreographer must find another composer to arrange and orchestrate these separate pieces into one whole; his problem here is to choose a live composer who likes and is sympathetic to the work of the dead one, so that there is no distortion of the original style and feeling. Among the classics *Les Sylphides* is the prime example of this method; the music is a selection of Chopin's piano pieces, carefully chosen by the choreographer and orchestrated by different composers. Some have done the job better than others.

In every ballet the story, or idea, the music, the scenery, the costumes, and the dancing should be in complete harmony in both style and atmosphere, otherwise the ballet cannot be entirely successful, however grand its intention.

A question which is very often asked is 'How are ballets written down?' Unfortunately, they are not. There is no way of putting a ballet on record, apart from actually filming it. There have been attempts to invent a notation, like the notation for music, but none has yet caught on. In America there is a new method beginning to make headway which may prove a blessing, but at present it is quite impossible in this country to record a modern ballet's enormous range of intricate movement. The classics can be recorded more easily because they are simpler in design and the steps are all straight from the old classical vocabulary and so can be written down in their original French names; when, in addition, the floor pattern is drawn out as it is executed to each phrase of the music and a note made of the style, some track may be kept of them.

But even the classics have never been written down in their original detail. These ballets have been handed down from dancer to dancer, which accounts for the differences to be seen in the same ballets as danced by different companies. The number of 'original' versions of the classics to be seen nowadays is amazing.

Even choreographers cannot be trusted to remember their own works, or perhaps to read their own notes, and revivals are seldom the same as the originals. All this goes to show that ballet is a very transient art indeed, and the masterpieces of one generation may well become the bores of the next, through misinterpretation or mis-remembering. It is a very great pity and I hope that such a state of affairs may alter in time to preserve some of the fine ballets of to-day accurately and in their entirety.

This book has dealt only with various aspects of the classical ballet, but it is from the old classical ballet that all other ballet has grown. To-day there is an enormously wide range of movements available to the choreographer, and a 'modern ballet' can cover almost any style or subject. Some would appear to disown their own ancestry, but then, how many of us can recognize our grandfathers in the picture in the family album of the baby kicking on the hearthrug?

If you see any ballet, classical or otherwise, that you don't like, don't condemn all ballet off-hand. There may have been so many reasons why you didn't like it; the dancers may not have been up to scratch, the music may have been badly played or at the wrong tempos, the choreography may not have been your cup of tea. It may not have been good.

But if you did enjoy it, it probably was good!

Other Books on the Dance

GORDON ANTHONY'S
Margot Fonteyn

Introduction by Dame Ninette de Valois, D.B.E.

4th impression. 15s. net

Limited edition in buckram boards, each copy signed by Margot Fonteyn and Gordon Anthony
63s. net

This is the first of a series of ballet books priced for the modest purse. That the distinguished names of Margot Fonteyn, Ninette de Valois and Gordon Anthony are here associated is sufficient guarantee that quality has not been sacrificed to price.

This book contains sixty studies in monochrome, with a colour frontispiece and wrapper. The pictures are selected from those taken by Gordon Anthony from the earlier days of Miss Fonteyn's career with the Sadlers Wells Ballet, at the age of 15 in 1935 in "The Haunted Ballroom", up to her creation of the part of Dulcinea for Miss de Valois' "Don Quixote" in 1950.

The descriptive captions to the pictures show the interesting progress of a young dancer as a soloist to the pinnacle of fame.

"This book is going on my shelves for permanent retention, as it makes a most attractive volume of reference."—*Dancing Times.*

"A book in which all lovers of the ballet will find delight."—*The Music Teacher.*

Royal 8vo. (10 × 6¼). 130 pp., including 60 pp. unbacked plates and colour frontispiece.
Full cloth boards.

GORDON ANTHONY'S
Alicia Markova

With an Appreciation by Dame Adeline Genée, D.B.E.

15s. net

Limited edition in leather case: signed by Alicia Markova and Gordon Anthony.   63s. net.

In three superb full colour portraits and 48 black and white studies Gordon Anthony presents a biography in photographs of England's first universally acknowledged *prima ballerina assoluta.*

Mr. Anthony's preface and detailed captions have a quality of personal enthusiasm which emphasizes the successive achievements of the little girl who was Alicia Marks, dancing Stravinsky's *Le Rossignol* for Diaghilev in Monte Carlo, who became the world-famous Markova of the first full-length *Lac des Cygnes* at Sadlers Wells and who will always be a legendary figure in ballet history.

Included in the book are plates of Markova in many roles which she created in this country, some of them with her famous partner, Dolin.

There is a historical appreciation by Dame Adeline Genée, the President of the Royal Academy of Dancing, who has followed, almost from the beginning, the career of this ballerina who over many years has never been equalled as a *danseuse sentimentale*.

Royal 8vo. (10 × 6¼). 118 pp., including 50 black and white and 3 colour unbacked plates. Full cloth boards.

RAM GOPAL
and SEROZH DADACHANJI

Indian Dancing

16s. net

'What Segovia is to the guitar and Casals to the 'cello, Gopal is to Indian dancing—a past master and the finest living exponent." The judgment is that of *The Stage*. With the collaboration of Serozh Dadachanji he has written this rich and beautiful record of the dance in India. It provides the Western reader with an easily understood account of the symbolism and sources of inspiration of one of the most lovely dance dramas in the world. In Indian dancing the smallest gesture has significance, and this fascinating book explains the language of the four schools of Indian dancing. The book is very fully illustrated with magnificent photographs from the authors' collections: many of these pictures have not been seen outside India. "Of exceptional importance."—*The Listener*.

Royal 8vo. (10 × 6¼). Full cloth boards.

ARNOLD HASKELL'S

Going to the Ballet

3rd impression   8s. 6d. net

The Director and Principal of Sadler's Wells Ballet School, and ballet's most widely read author, here introduces the younger generation (aged 12-16) to the delights of watching ballet, an undertaking for which he is particularly well fitted since he has talked to hundreds of schools on the subject. Presenting ballet first as a whole, Mr. Haskell then takes it apart and examines separately its ingredients of dancing, music, drama and choreography. He covers an immense amount of ground, from the origins of dancing to the place of ballet on the world's stages to-day, and in films and television.

The forty-three photographs include unique examples from the author's own collection.

"There could not be a more attractive book on ballet."—*The Star*.

Crown 8vo. (7½ × 5). 43 plates. Full cloth boards.

These books are published by Phoenix House Ltd., 38 William IV St. Charing Cross, London, W.C. 2